GALVESTON

ISLAND OF CHANCE

BY

FRANK E. CHALFANT

GALVESTON ISLAND OF CHANCE

Published by: Treasures of Nostalgia
10035 Kemp Forest Dr.
Houston, Texas 77080-2601
713-460-9244

Library of Congress Catalog Card Number: 97-90783

ISBN: 0-9659566-0-1

Printed in the United States of America

Printed by Technigrafiks Inc: Houston, Texas

DEDICATION

This book is dedicated to all those that have gone before me; to those that are here with me now; and to those that will be here after I have gone.

AUTHOR'S NOTES

My quest began, by chance, ten years ago when I acquired an antique slot machine. I had heard stories about the illegal gambling in Galveston, so on one of my visits to the island I thought I would try to find some of the old gambling chips. After finding a few chips, I discovered some of them had the initials TAC and BR. I knew that BR was for the Balinese Room, but I didn't know what the TAC stood for. After some research, I discovered that it stood for the Turf Athletic Club. Later I found more chips, but the problem was, there were new names and initials that were unknown to me. That meant more research, then more new chips and more research. My research continues, because I am still finding new, unidentified chips.

My research has been by taped interviews with people that have been involved in the history making events and with employees that worked in the clubs, as they were called then. The word "casino" meant gambling and even though it was wide open, gambling was not publicity advertised. It was just a known fact that most of the clubs had gambling of some type. It may have been only a few slot machines and a blackjack table, but they had it. Some of my other sources have been old magazines and news papers, city directories, books, periodicals, libraries and tax court records and other collectors. I have attempted, to best of my ability, to convey the information and identify the items as accurately as possible. When possible, I have obtained more than one verification. If you have any additions or corrections, please forward them to me, along with your source.

I am currently president of the *Greater Houston Casino Chip and Gaming Token Collectors.* We hold monthly meetings in Houston, where we identify and trade newly discovered chips. We have members that also collect newer issue casino chips and tokens form around the world.

Unless otherwise noted, all items illustrated are from my personal collection. I do have some duplicates that are available for private acquisition. If you would like to own a piece of Galveston history, you can reach me through the publisher. Please send a SASE along with your wish list. I am always looking for new items from the Galveston area to add to my private collection. If you have any items you think may be of interest to me, please contact me with their descriptions.

To the lucky people who have had the good fortune to have been entertained in those magnificent, legendary, establishments, I hope you find this book a medium to transport you back to that nostalgic period of grandeur. It is my sincere wish that you find this book, enjoyable, informative, and a genuine page turner.

The flower blooms, the fruit ripens, and the baby takes its first steps. All too soon these things change. If the flower is not looked upon, the fruit not eaten, nor the baby loved, you will miss your chance. They will be gone forever. So take the time to smell the roses, enjoy the fruits of your labor, and hug that child, for far too soon, they will be like the fabulous places I have written about, they will be gone.

I researched, authored, edited, did the photographic and graphic work, designed, assembled, and published this book. It is not like any other book, but then, it is not supposed to be. If I may coin the words in a song, sung by one of the people that helped make Galveston famous, Frank Sinatra, "I did it my way."

If you find mistakes in this book, please consider that they are there for a purpose. I wanted to publish something for everyone and some people are always looking for mistakes!!!

ACKNOWLEDGEMENT AND SOURCES

I wish to offer my sincere gratitude and heartfelt thanks to the following authors, journalists, historians, publications, articles, and fellow collectors. A special thanks to the individuals who were part of the making of history making events, that were gracious enough to grant me an interview; James P. Simpson, Pinky Hull, Angelo Montalbano, Angelo Tramuto, Paul Berlin, Linda Mendez, Ellabeth Hencey, Steve Dowell, A. Pat Daniels, Dale Roberts, and Vic A. Maceo Jr.

It is my sorrowful duty to report the passing of Walter Douglas "Pinky" Hull, Jr. He was born May 23, 1926 and went to play his "Plinkety-Plink" piano for the Lord on April 17, 1997. Heaven will be a more lively place, now that you are there.

My deepest gratitude to the Rosenberg Library, Galveston; Casey Edward Green, Anna B. Peebler, and Shelly Henley Kelly. I would also like to thank; Vern Blanck, Doc Finstuen, Sandra Thompson, John Scardino, Dan Castillo, Tony Cisneros, and the many others that we kind enough to let me illustrate items from their collections and supply me with useful bits of information.

To my wife Ellen, who gave up part of her newly remodeled kitchen for my office and the year and a half of my time I spent writing. Also for her eagle eye that spotted those Galveston items that I missed while we were antiquing.

Ray Miller's Galveston: Second edition, by Ray Miller.
Galveston: a History of the Island, by Gary Cartwright.
Is there a Leprechaun in the Gazebo?, by Pinky Hull.
From Tent Show to Opera, by Pinky Hull. Peninsula Press of Texas, P. O. Box 694, Houston, Texas 77001
Galveston, by Charles W. Hayes.
Tempo Sunday Magazine, August 3, 1969.

The Gamblers, Time-Life Books.
Life Magazine, June 19, 1950.
Galveston City Directory, 1928-29, 1930, 1934-35, 1951, 1955.
The Houston Post.
The Houston Chronicle.
The Texas City Sun.
Texas Monthly Magazine.
The Galveston Daily News.
The Daily News, Galveston County.
Isle of Illicit Pleasures Series, by Alan Waldman.
In Between Magazine.
The Galvez and the Gambling Years, by Janice Williams.
A Time Past: Gambling in Galveston. by Henry David.
The Island and City of Galveston,
Tax Court Memorandum Decisions, Commerce Clearing House Inc.
Galveston: A History, by David G. McComb.
The Lonely Star: Texas Confidential.
Aces High: The Maceo Legend, by Jennifer Kelso.
End of Gambling Era Hits Home, by Therese Deats.
This Week in Galveston, by Garry Pliner.
Galveston Week, by Christie Mitchell.
Galveston Isle, by Galveston Isle Publishing Company Inc.

CONTENTS

BACKWARD

Galveston has gone by many names over the course of history. In 1528 some charts and journals used by Cabeza de Vaca referred to it as *Malhado,* others charts called it *Lsla de Culebras, "Island of Snakes,"* due to the large quantity of snakes on the island. By 1783 the Spanish navigator Hervia had named the bay Galvez Bay, in honor of Mexico's viceroy Don Bernardo de Galvez. Eventually it became known as Galveston Bay and Galvezton became known as Galveston. Around 1817, Jean Laffite and his brother Pierre, called their camp Campeche, also spelled Campeachy.

Galveston has also been called other names such as *"New York of the Gulf,"* "*Wall Street of the Southwest," "Ellis Island of the West," "The Big Sand Bar," "Island City," "Port and Playground of the Southwest," "The South's Treasure Island on the Gulf of Mexico," "The Sportsman's Paradise," "The Treasure Island of America," "The Free State of Galveston,*" and to the lucky people who live there, it's called Home! I prefer to think of it as *ISLAND OF CHANCE.* To me, Galveston is truly an island of chance.

Four and a half billion years ago when the *Big Bang* created our solar system and third rock from the sun, the place we all call home, Jimmy "The Greek" Snyder, couldn't have given the odds that this little island would be so important to the history of the United States and the World. For the souls of the 6000 men, women, and children that lost their lives in the 15 hour long, September 8 & 9, 1900 hurricane, the odds were stacked heavily against them.

There have been many foot prints left in the sand on the island. Early man, called Paleoindians, migrated across the land bridge from Siberia in the Bering Strait around thirteen thousand years ago. Since the last "Ice Age" ended ten thousand years ago, some of them may have settled in the Southwest and might have visited the island, but there is no evidence to substantiate this. It should be noted that there was a "Little Ice Age" from 1550 to 1850. The first known people to occupy the island on a large scale were the cannibalistic Karankawa and the Akikosa Indian tribes.

Many important men and women have visited or lived on the island and have left their marks in the annals of history. Frank and Jesse James lived in Galveston for five months in 1874 with their wives Annie Walston and Zeralda Mimms. On the run again they moved to Nashville, Tennessee. Jesse was shot in the back on April 3, 1882 in St. Joseph, Missouri by his outlaw friend Charlie Ford. Charlie and his brother Bob were paid $10,000 each, plus a full governor's pardon, by Mr. Pinkerton for their deed. On October 10, 1882, Frank was charged with a wide array of crimes, but was acquitted three times and never served a day in jail. How would the history of Galveston changed if they hadn't moved away?

There are foot prints that will never be found, those of the gigantic dinosaurs. When the one hundred and eighty million year reign of the dinosaurs began around two hundred and fifty million years ago, what is now North America's southern coastline and the grains of sand that make up Galveston, were in the middle of a super continent called Pangaea, "all earth," that was located on the equator. The North American tectonic plate moved northwestwardly about one mile every thirty thousand years to its present location.

The Cosmic Zap, an impact meteor, approximately six miles in diameter, traveling fifty thousand miles an hour, struck Chicxulub, Yucatan with a force of one-hundred million megaton of *TNT,* sixty-five million years ago. The asteroid created a gigantic crater one hundred thirty miles across, about the size of Connecticut, and twenty five hundred feet deep. The impact caused a tidal wave that threw three foot diameter boulders, two hundred miles up the Brazos River. It also created the *Z-COAL* line, which contains Iridium, tektites, shocked quartz, and soot. Iridium is an element that is rare on earth but plentiful in asteroids. It is also known as the *K-T* boundary. It separates the Cretaceous and the Tertiary periods and can be found around the world. The school is still out on exactly what caused the mass extinction of the dinosaurs and other ancient life forms in the seas. It is believed by many Paleontologists that this event led to their extinction. The latest evidence of the enormous power of these impacts, comes from meteorites, recently found in Antarctica, that were propelled into space by an asteroid impacts on Mars. There is also a theory, that not all of the dinosaurs became extinct, but that some may have evolved to become your Sunday chicken dinner. The Chicxulub meteor was two hundred and twenty times larger than the one that struck Meteor Crater, Arizona between 45,000 and 50,000 years ago. The Arizona meteor was a mere one hundred and fifty feet across, but made a crater almost one mile in diameter and 640 feet deep.

When the last mighty T-Rex took its final hot steamy breath some sixty-five million years ago, it was not on Galveston Island, nor was it any where close. At that point in time, a shallow sea, five hundred feet deep, called the Cretaceous Seaway, divided the North American continent in half. It went from the Texas coast up to Alaska. It could have happened in Texas, but it would have had to have been in Central Texas or the West Texas hill country.

All of the above are worthy of their own chapters or even their own books, but this is not what my book is about. Mine is the story of the gambling era in Galveston and the surrounding locality.

SONGS OF GALVESTON

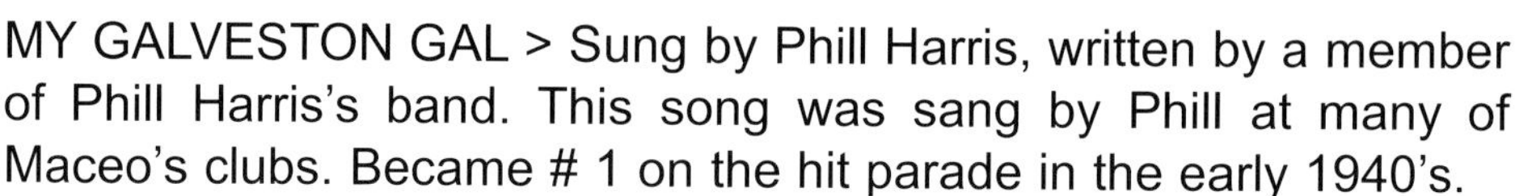

MY GALVESTON GAL > Sung by Phill Harris, written by a member of Phill Harris's band. This song was sang by Phill at many of Maceo's clubs. Became # 1 on the hit parade in the early 1940's.

MY GALAVANTIN' GALVESTON GAL > Sung by Gene Autry composed at the request of the Greater Galveston Beach Association in the mid 1940's.

GALVESTON > Sung by Glen Campbell. Glen sang of the sea breeze blowing and the sea wall.

BALINESE > Sung by ZZ Top, lyrics told of drinking whisky and rolling dice at the Balinese Room.

THE FAMILY

SAM & ROSE'S MOTHER:
Angelina Maceo.

SAM & ROSE'S FATHER:
Vito Maceo.

SAM MACEO:
Salvatore Maceo born March 1, 1894, died April 16, 1951 of cancer at Johns Hopkins Hospital. Sam's first wife, Jessica McBride, divorced November 8, 1941. Married second wife Edna Sedgewick December 29, 1941. Edna married Henry G. Plitt, partner of the movie chain. Edna was listed as Sam's widow in 1955 Galveston city directory.

SAM MACEO'S TWIN SONS:
Victor Edward Maceo (Eddie) & Salvatore Maceo (Jay-R) born August 18, 1942.

SAM MACEO's DAUGHTER:
Edna Sedgewick Maceo (Sedgie) born August 18, 1944.

ROSE MACEO:
Rosario Maceo born September 8, 1887 died March 15, 1954 of heart trouble. Rose's first wife was murdered. Married second wife Frances Dispensa September 1922. Frances' mother Frances Jessica, father Angelo Santo. Frances listed as Rose's widow 1955 Galveston city directory.

ROSE MACEO'S SON:
Rosario Maceo Jr. adopted 1951.

SAM & ROSE'S BROTHER:
Vincent C. Maceo.

VINCENT C. MACEO'S DAUGHTER:
Anglia.

SAM & ROSE'S BROTHER:
Frank Maceo.

SAM & ROSE'S SISTER:
Olivia, married Frank Fertitta.

FRANK MACEO'S SON:
Rosario S. (Rose) (R. S. Maceo) (Slick) President R. S. Maceo Seafood Inc. was not into the gambling. Wife Dorothy, son Ronnie.

FRANK MACEO'S SON:
Vincent A. Maceo born January 27, 1914 in New Orleans, La. Married O. E. (Dutch) Voight's daughter Estelle June 1, 1939. Divorced November 1951. She later became Estelle Maceo Parmer. Vincent then married Angie.

FRANK MACEO'S SON:
Joe T. Maceo.

FRANK MACEO'S DAUGHTER:
Florence married Robert Lee Fabj, (Babby) (1920/1996).

FRANK MACEO'S DAUGHTER:
Concetta (Chatta) married John B. Arena.
(Albert A. Arena was a maintenance man for Gulf Properties).

SAM & ROSE'S NEPHEW :
Vic A. Maceo (Gigolo) wife Thelma, son Vic A. Maceo Jr.

SAM & ROSE'S FIRST COUSINS:
(Brothers) Frank Maceo wife Katherine, Vic C. Maceo (Little Vic) wife Katie, Samuel T. Maceo (Sam T.) (S. T.) (Little Sammy) wife Dorothy.

ALSO LISTED IN 1955 GALVESTON CITY DIRECTORY:
Joseph A. Maceo, wife Pearl, Maceo & Co.
Mrs. Anna Maceo.

FRANK & OLIVIA (MACEO) FERTITTA'S SON:
Victor J. Fertitta wife Mary (Falco).

VICTOR J. FERTITTA'S CHILDREN:
Olivia, J. V. later changed his name to V. J. (Vic) Fertitta.

V. J. (Vic) FERTITTA'S CHILDREN:
Tilman, Todd, and Jay one of their wive's maiden name was Falco.

FRANK & OLIVIA (MACEO) FERTITTA'S SON:
Anthony J. Fertitta wife LaVella.

FRANK & OLIVIA (MACEO) FERTITTA'S SON:
Frank J. Fertitta wife Deady, later ran Place Station in Las Vegas.

FRANK J. FERTITTA'S CHILDREN:
Olivia, Joe, and Linda.

FRANK & OLIVIA (MACEO) FERTITTA'S SON:
Tom A. Fertitta (Tommie) wife Concetta.

FRANK & OLIVIA (MACEO) FERTITTA'S SON:
Sam Fertitta wed 1946.

FRANK & OLIVIA (MACEO) FERTITTA'S SON:
Joe Fertitta.

FRANK & OLIVIA (MACEO) FERTITTA'S DAUGHTER:
Olivia.

ALSO LISTED IN 1955 GALVESTON CITY DIRECTORY:
Betty J. Fertitta ,Frank Jr. Fertitta, Joe S. Fertitta wife Sue.

O. E. (DUTCH) VOIGH:
Born Nov. 18, 1888, in Brenham, TX. Married Bessie Downey. divorced between 1923 & 1925.

O. E. (DUTCH) VOIGH MARRIED CHILDREN'S NAMES:
Bessie Cripps, Estelle (Maceo) Parmer, Margaret Williams.

RELATED BY MARRIAGE:
Sam (Books) Serio wife Pearl M. from Beaumont, brother Vincent S. Serio wife Kate A., Arthur J. (Yak) Adams, wife Maude.
There were countless other relatives and in-laws in the business.

MACEO'S HOLDINGS

Owned, owned stock, or invested in.

Turf Athletic Club 8/6/32 Partnership > Rose, Sam, Voight, Frank and D. D. Alexander
The Hollywood Sui-Jen Dinner Club 1936 Partnership > Sam, Rose, Voight, and Quinn
The Hollywood Dinner Club
The Grotto
The Sui Jen
The Chop Suey
The Derby Amusement Co. Inc. 1937
Gulf Properties Inc. 1938
Beach Amusement Park Inc. 1939
Miss Hollywood Inc. 1941
Galveston Pier Corp. Inc. 1947
Galveston Isle Publishing Co. Inc. 1947
Murdoch Bath House Co. Inc. 1914
Galveston Pleasure Pier Inc. 1916
Vernell Liquor Co. Partnership
San Luis Corp. Inc.
Play Land Amusement Co.
R. Maceo And Co.
Maceo And Co.
M. and M. Building Corp.
M. and M. Music Co.
Modern Music Co.
R. S. Maceo Seafoods Inc.
Turf Grill
True Tap Room
Studio Lounge
Western Room
Horse Operations

Lay-off Betting
Turf Cigar Stand
Home Plate Cigar Stand
Balinese Room
Beach Club
Bird Cage
Crystal Sports land # 1
Crystal Sports land # 2
Crystal Palace
Turf Stores
Stewart Beach Catering Co.
Maceo Catering Co.
The Fish House
Gulf Room
The Corner
Park Portland
Yacht Balinese
Chili Bowl
Moulin Rouge Club
Streamline Dinner Club
Edgewater Lounge
Silver Moon
Gulf Vending Co.
Dickinson Equipment Co.
Galveston Novelty Co.
Stewart Beach
Sam Maceo Oil Operations
General Crude Oil Co.
Kemah Den
Marine Room
Sportsmans Club

THE HISTORY

It is not known exactly when the first gambling took place on Galveston Island, but when the first two men set foot on the island, you can be certain that one of them bet the other one that he could run faster or throw a clam shell farther. Gambling is one of mankind's oldest forms of entertainment. Every country and nationality had their own methods of gambling. Aboriginal Indian tribes had many types of games of chance and were addicted to betting as a sacred ritual. Early explorers, smugglers, pirates, and sailors had their own modes of gambling. Many of which are still in use today with just a few modifications.

Toward the end of 1838 and the beginning of 1839, gamblers poured into Galveston from New Orleans, Houston, and other cities with the intention of fleecing the unsuspecting immigrants from their money and leaving them with jack squat, in a strange new land. They came with their tents and gambling paraphernalia, ready to set up shop on vacant lots near any main road. In 1839, the City Council introduced an ordinance for the suppression of gambling, that read, in part, as follows:

"Whereas, The City Council looks upon the practice of gambling as one having the most pernicious and demoralizing influence in the community; and deeming it the duty of all constituted authorities to employ the most efficient means to carry into effect the strictness of the law already enacted upon the subject by the National Congress, therefore, be it."

"*Resolved*, That twenty men (or as many more as the Mayor may deem necessary), as special constables, be appointed to cooperate with the present existing authorities, in order to more effectually suppress gambling in the city of Galveston."

The City Council held such a strict regard for Sunday that on May 16, 1840, they appointed a committee to draft an ordinance, that read, in part, as follows:

"Be it ordained, that no person shall be allowed to play at the games of billiards, or nine- or ten-pins, during the Sabbath day or night, within the limits of the corporation, under a penalty of not less than ten nor more than one hundred dollars for each and every offense."

Regardless of the stringent ordinances adopted by the first Council, the succeeding Council, in August 1840, adopted a more rigorous ordinance, that read, in part, as follows:

"To prohibit and restrain gambling," the first section of which sets forth, "that it shall not be lawful, from and after the publication of this ordinance, for any person or persons to play with cards or dice, or any faro-bank, or any gaming table by whatsoever name, title or figure the same may be distinguished or known, or at any game of chance for money or other valuable thing, within the limits of said city."

It was also unlawful for any "person or persons to bet or wager money, or other valuable thing, on the ticket or hands of such as do game with cards or dice, or at any faro-bank, or at any gaming table as aforesaid." The penalty for committing either of the above offenses was $50 for each offense, and the offender, moreover, could be made to execute a bond, with good and acceptable security, for "his good behavior, for a term not exceeding twelve months, in any sum not exceeding $500." This bond was demanded by the Recorder whenever he had a doubt that the offender would again violate the ordinance. In case any person or persons so offending, and who refused to pay, or were unable to pay, or who refused to give, or were unable to procure, a bond, they were committed to prison, until released by due course of law.

There were similar ordinances that dealt with licensed boarding houses, taverns, and hotel operators, or retailers of ardent spirits prohibiting the keeping or exhibiting any gaming table, of any name or description whatsoever. "Any person engaged in selling liquor or intoxicating spirits to the slaves without an order from their owners, was assessed a heavy fine and their license was revoked." There was another ordinance against all vagrants, idle or disorderly persons of evil life, or ill-fame with no visible means of support, found drunk, begging, loitering, or grossly indecent in language or behavior in the streets.

I realize the preceding was a little dry reading, but I wanted to emphasize that the City Fathers were trying to make Galveston a goody-two-shoes city. Remember, this was just four years after the fall of the Alamo and the declaration of independence for Republic of Texas from Mexico, five years before statehood, and twenty years before the beginning of the Civil War. Galveston had seventy years to wait for the arrival of the Maceos.

A grand jury in November 1901 reported there were a few old-established gambling houses in the city that were ran in a quiet manner with no complaints of any kind. There were two establishments in the city that had been in operation for some years and that they had forty-three branches or shops spread around the town. The jury was advised that these places no longer permitted children to patronize them. They were also provided a list of fifty-seven places where nickel-in-the-slot machines, (an early term for slot machines), were being exhibited and played. They also found, as with any seaport, a large number of dives. These places contain saloons, dance halls, gambling, etc., and are frequented by a disorderly class of both white and black, male and female, many of whom are either petty thieves or common vagrants. They found that while they cannot be entirely suppressed, they can and should be regulated by the police and placed thoroughly under the control of the law.

Salvatore (Sam) Maceo and his older brother Rosario (Rose) Maceo were born in Palermo, Sicily and immigrated to the lumber town of Leesville, Louisiana with their parents in 1900. They moved to Galveston in 1910 and their first employment was as barbers at Cappadona's at 25th and Market Street. Sam then became a barber at the Galvez Hotel when it opened in 1911 and Rose cut hair on Murdoch's Pier.

The Maceos did not start the rackets. Gambling, prostitution, smuggling, bootlegging, and rumrunning have always flourished in Galveston. As with any vice the government seems to make it prosper. In 1919, prohibition gave the gangsters an opportunity to make fortunes running rum and bootlegging. The hooch was off-loaded outside the three-mile limit from schooners that sailed from ports in the Bahamas, Cuba, Jamaica, or British Honduras. The ships would carry between 2,000 and 20,000 cases of brand-name liquor. A bootlegger could make $10,000 to $300,000, post World War I money, on each shipment. They supplied illegal booze to Southwest and Midwest. This thriving operation lasted until the repeal of the Eighteenth Amendment in 1933 when Congress modified the Volstead Act and permitted the sale of 3.2 beer, but it was still unlawful to sell liquor by the drink in Texas. With the federal prohibition repealed, Texans voted in 1935 to allow the sale of liquor in package stores.

There were two gangs that ran the operations on the island,

with Broadway being the dividing line. The Beach Gang operated the south side of the island and was ramrodded by Ollie J. Quinn and his cohort, Dutch Voight. The north side was controlled by the Downtown Gang. It was command by George Musey and John L. "Johnny Jack" Nounes, aka, "The Beau Brummel of Galveston."

The Maceos got started in the rumrunning business when Rose was approached by Voight. If Rose could hide 1,500 cases of liquor under his beach cottage, they were willing pay him $1 a case for his trouble. This was good money. Rose was cutting hair for 25¢ at the time. After the contraband was picked up a few days later, Voight came by to pay Rose his $1,500. Rose told him, "Instead of paying me, you can keep the money and let me in on your next shipment." Voight and Quinn agreed to let Rose in on the next acquisition. Soon the Maceos were into the bootlegging business. One of their favorite caches was a swampy thicket at 61st Street and Stewart Road, where the K Mart store is now located and across the street for where the Hollywood Dinner Club would later be built.

Johnny Jack was the most ostentatious of the bootleggers. He was up before Judge Joseph C. Hutcheson Jr., where he had appeared many times on the charge of bootlegging. The judge fined him $5,000 for this offense. Johnny Jack smiled at the judge and said, "Hell Judge, I've got that much here in my right-hand pocket." "Then reach into your left-hand pocket," the judge responded "and see if you can find two years in the penitentiary in there." Johnny Jack spent the next two years in the gray-bar hotel, as a guest of the federal prison system. Another time the federal authorities were searching for him and had sealed off the bus and train stations. Johnny Jack had a gait that was similar to Charlie Chaplin. He bought a bowler, dark suit and cane, put on a moustache, and waddled right past the feds, thus eluding his pursuers.

The Coast Guard used to scout the Gulf from atop the Buccaneer Hotel, looking for rumrunners' boats. One night the Beach Gang was bringing a boatload of whiskey to the island when something didn't jibe, and they became leery of the Coast Guard. They took the boat to the oyster reefs on the west end of the island and scuttled it. Upon returning the next night to retrieve the hooch out of the sunken vessel, they discovered some of their cache had drifted away. For weeks and months to come, beachcombers were astonished and delighted by the bottles of Canadian Club whiskey that would wash ashore with the tides.

There's a story about a boat from Cuba that came to Galveston with a load of illegal rum. After their cargo had been unloaded, they swiftly steamed back home to Havana. Somewhere between Galveston and Havana the Cubans discovered that instead of being paid in greenbacks, they had been paid off with worthless soap coupons. There is no account of who pulled off the scam, but you can bet the ranch, that they were the cleanest Cubans in Havana for some time to come.

A youthful lad named Frank Noonis, who was born Francesco Raffaele Nitti, was living at the Galvez Hotel and was in partnership with Johnny Jack Nounes and Dutch Voight. Frank made an unscheduled relocation to Chicago with an old steamer trunk containing $24,000 that belonged to Johnny and Dutch. In Chicago, Nitti became the infamous, Frank "The Enforcer" Nitti, strong arm and chief executioner of the untouchable fame, Al "Scarface" Capone. Frank had been seen drinking with cronies in a Houston speakeasy one evening. Dutch and Johnny snatched Nitti and whisk back to the island where his two ex-partners explained to him over a plate of spaghetti, that spaghetti wouldn't be the best choice, for a last meal. Frank got the message and was permitted to return to Chicago after he returned the $24,000, plus interest.

Sam and Rose opened a barbershop after the war and began giving some Dago Red to their good patrons around the holidays. Soon the customers were wanting more. In 1921 Sam opened a cold drink place and began to sell liquor. Ollie J. Quinn agreed to share some of his gambling territory with the Maceos.

In 1923 Sam and Rose made their first attempt into the entertainment business when they opened the Chop Suey at 21st and Seawall Boulevard. The Chop Suey can be seen in a 1924, wide-angle photograph of Murdoch's Bathhouse, at Gaido's Seafood Restaurant, in the hallway, opposite their gift shop. Sam, Rose, and Voight renamed it the Maceo's Grotto in 1926. The Grotto was closed in 1928 for a gaming violation, then was damaged by a storm in 1932. Remodeled and renamed the Sui Jen, (pronounced Swee Wren), it reopened in 1932 with an Oriental decor. In February 1942, after being remodeled again this time with a South Seas setting, it was given the name Balinese Room. Some say it was changed from an Oriental to a South Seas decor because of the bombing of Pearl Harbor by Japan on December 7, 1941. The Balinese Room still sets on barnacle-covered pilings, at the end of a long pier, above the blue waters of the Gulf of Mexico. It always had a guard posted at the front entrance to screen the patrons and issue membership card to those who they wanted to enter and to warn of unwanted visitors. The long pier that isolated the Balinese Room from the Seawall Boulevard quickly became known as, "The Ranger Run." By the

FEC # 1 Balinese Room from post card, circa 1950's.

time the law enforcement officers reached the restaurant and the windowless back gambling room, the illegal gambling paraphernalia had been hidden. From manager to busboy, each had a designated assignment during a raid. The roulette wheels were lifted out and the side-together tables were put into hidden panels in the walls. Dice layouts were wrapped up and transformed to billiard tables. Suitcases full of gambling chips were passed through a half-door in back of the bar into the kitchen. Once a bewildered cook hid a suitcase in a still hot oven and ruined a complete set of chips. This had to be the first attempt at oven baked chips. A complete change from casino to a recreation room took only thirty seconds. Occasionally the customers would pitch in and help the staff hide the equipment. No Texas Ranger ever made it to the back room before the goodies had been stashed. It is said that when there was a raid in a Maceo club, the band performing there had standing orders to strike up *The Eyes of Texas Are Upon You,* all the patriotic patrons would rise, thereby blocking the aisles, slowing the Rangers race to the back rooms. The local police had a very complacent attitude. They reacted when there was a complaint and very few people complained. When Sheriff Frank Biaggne was ask by a Senate Committee on Crime in Austin why he didn't raid the Balinese Room. "They won't let me in," he said, "I'm not a member."

Also in 1926 Sam, Rose, Voight, and Quinn opened the island's first big time club, the fabulous, air-conditioned, Hollywood Dinner Club at 6102 Avenue S, (Stewart Road) at 61st Street, just outside the Galveston city limits. It had a large searchlight that would shine into the sky that could be seen for miles. The temperature at the Maceo clubs was always kept at 69°. This was not only for the comfort of the patrons, but so they could drink more and feel it less. It had superb food, drinks, dancing, stellar entertainment, and best of all they had gambling. Sam had a policy that no patron should have to light their own cigarette. When you took out a smoke, the Johnny-on-the-spot wait staff, were at your table with a lit match. The Maceos booked many top stars in their clubs including Frank Sinatra, Sophie Tucker, Joe E. Lewis, the Ritz Brothers, Peggy Lee, Marjorie Reynolds, Phil Harris, and superb big bands such as Henry Busse, Isham Jones, Bob Crosby, Ben Pollack, Guy Lambardo and his Royal Canadians, Ted Mack, Jimmy Dorsey, Ted Weems, Shep Fields, Ray Noble, and Freddy Martin.

The Maceos made the Hollywood Dinner Club one of the best night spots in the nation. Sam and Rose were very intelligent entrepreneurs. They stayed away from prostitution and would not let shills anywhere near the clubs. A shill was a girl that would hang out with a customer encouraging him to drink and gambled. She would lead him to believe she was going to spend the night with him. She was served liquor-less drinks and received a cut from the gaming tables. When the night was drawing to an end she would do a fade from her mark and disappear. Rose was the tough business man and Sam possessed all the finesse. Sam became good friends with

FEC # 2 L To R: Anthony Fertitta, Jimmy Van Heusen, Frank Sinatra, and Sam Maceo in the Balinese Room. Galveston Isle Magazine. March, 1950.

and booked all the big names in the entertainment business. It is my heartfelt opinion that Sam Maceo was to Galveston, what Steve Wynn is to Las Vegas today. The Maceo organization had such accurate book keeping records, that the Las Vegas casinos would call them to check the credit rating of customers that were seeking gambling markers. The late "Little" Jakie Freedman, grandfather of Houston's prestigious River Oaks socialite and fund-raiser extraordinaire, Carolyn Farb, ran the dice game. He was an early investor in the Hollywood Dinner Club, but sold his interest to the original partners in 1927. After selling his investment, Freedman moved to Houston, where he later opened the elegant, "Domain Privee" in a colonial mansion, off South Main Street. When the gambling laws started being enforced in the early 1950's, he closed the Domain Privee, moved the Las Vegas where gambling was legal, and constructed the world famous Sands.

FEC # 3 Jakie Freedman's Domain Privee on South Main Street in Houston.

Galveston's large casinos in were not open to the general public. They were called private clubs. You had to be a member to enter, this enabled them to sell hard liquor by the drink, but this was still a violation of the law, even in a genuine club. You had to be a member, be known, or know somebody to be admitted. They didn't advertise gambling, but they didn't hide it either. Public officials and the lawmen claimed that the public wanted open gambling. God knows, they certainly had it. From the large clubs to the small bars, drugstores, coffee shops, and filling stations, most had slot machines, tip books, and punch boards. The Maceos discouraged locals from gambling in their larger clubs, win or lose, it was bad for business. However, local big gamblers W. L. Moody IV and Maco Stewart were always welcome. There were plenty of smaller places in town where the other locals could place a bet, play a tip book, or pull the handle of their favorite one armed bandit and chances were good that the machines were either owned or leased by the Maceo's Galveston Novelty Co. or the Dickinson Equipment Co., in which they had a 75% interest.

Illegal gambling was a big business in almost every in state in America in the first half of the century. In a June 19, 1950 issue of *Life Magazine,* there was a twenty-two page article on *Gambling in the U. S.* that did not mention Galveston, nor any other city in Texas. Maybe it was because *Life* was published in Chicago, Illinois? Gambling was wide spread throughout Texas, but no place could hold a candle to the legendary, *Free State of Galveston*.

By the early 1930's most of the Downtown Gang either was in the hoosegow, bought out, or had been persuaded to leave town. Ollie Quinn took over the operations for a while but it wasn't long before the Maceos were in charge of it all. There were other small time operators on the island, but they were allowed to do business by the grace of Big Sam and Papa Rose. Rose ruled with an iron fist. Sam managed with a velvet glove.

Sam "Books" Serio came to Galveston in 1934, during the depression, but he said you could hardly tell, with all the money that was flying around, that there was a depression going on. One year during the 30's, business started getting a little slow. Sam and Rose asked their employees to take a pay cut from $125 to $75 a week. They promised that if they had a good year they'd make it up to them. Sure enough, they had a great season and large bonuses were received by all.

The Turf Athletic Club (TAC) was the holding company for the Maceo family. It maintained offices on the first and third floors at the Turf Grill building, with a staff of eight to ten. It was a three-story building on two adjoining lots at 2214 and 2216 Market, between 23rd and Postoffice. The first floor was occupied by a bistro, the Turf Tap Room, and an eatery, the Turf Grill, a pool hall, tip counter, and a mezzanine. There were two offices on the first floor that adjoined the check cashing booth. The first office was called the counting room. The second office, contained two safes, and the first floor offices of Joe T. Maceo and Sam Serio. It was referred to as the safe room. The second floor, who's only access was by a very slow elevator equipped with an alarm buzzer, housed the luxurious Studio Lounge, horse room and card room, and the Turf Club. On the third floor was the Western Room, which was known for its western decor, an athletic club complete with a regulation size boxing ring, and a poolroom. It also contained a large room for the accounting department, a smaller office shared by Joe T. Maceo and Sam Serio, plus rooms used for other designated purposes. The Turf had been wrecked by Rangers in 1935 and had to be redecorated. There was an electric eye on the door for a while, but people kept going in and out the wrong door and kept getting hit by the door. It was removed and replaced by the first revolving door in Texas. The Turf Grill building was razed in the 1970's and a new large bank building was constructed on the lots.

The Maceo empire grew over the years to have holdings in many businesses both on and off the island. The Moodys, Sealys, and Kempners controlled most of the banking on the island, but the Maceos made loans to the smaller businesses who were sometimes unable to acquire loans at the bigger banks. The Turf Athletic Club soon became known as, "The Weekend Bank of Galveston." Businessmen could cash checks for thousands of dollars at the Turf on weekends. If the Maceos favored the business you wanted to start, or the improvements you wanted to made on your existing business, they would float you a loan with the understanding that Dickinson Equipment Co. or Galveston Novelty Co., that was overseen by John B. Arena, would be put their vending and slot machines in your place of business. Robert Lee Fabj supervised the collections that were made from the machines at least weekly. Before 1950 it was divided equally, after 1950 the cut was, Maceo 60%, location owner 40%. On collection day, the money would be counted immediately, reimbursements made for any refunds, then split according to the agreed percentages. A por-

FEC # 4 Mr. & Mrs. Vernon enter the Turf Grill through the revolving door. Galveston Isle Magazine. November, 1947.

tion of the merchants commission was applied toward the loan. In some locations the store owner would allow the entire amount to be applied to the loan. The amount that went for the loan was marked "stake" on the collection ticket and transferred to the company books by Sam Serio when it was turned into him at the Turf Grill building safe room each night.

The Maceos expanded into other businesses such as oil properties and real estate. If someone had a good location, as was the case with Fatty Owens, who had his own slot machines in the bar he operated, Gulf Properties, a Maceo holding company, bought the property, thus becoming the new landlord. His machines were removed and replaced with Maceo owned slot machines. The time soon came when the Maceos interests owned so much land in Galveston County that people traveling south to Galveston would say, as they crossed the Harris-Galveston County line, that they were crossing the "Maceo-Dickinson" line.

FEC # 5 L To R: Sam Maceo, Carmen Cavallaro, and Mayor Herbert Y. Cartwright Jr. at Studio Lounge, circa 1947-1955. Courtesy of Rosenberg Library, Galveston, Texas.

Betting operations by the Maceos were divided into five different categories. They were sporting events: horse racing, football, baseball, basketball, and games of chance. Maceos also made and accepted lay-off bets on scheduled sporting events. A lay-off bet arises when a bookmaker who accepted a bet determines that the risk involved therein is too great to be borne solely by himself. Arrangements are then made with another bookmaker to accept an agreed portion of the bet. After the event on which a lay-off bet is completed, a settlement is made by the bettor making the lay-off and the bettor accepting the lay-off. Bets could be made at most Maceo locations and they had arrangements with other proprietors for the placing of bets. They would receive a 25% commission on the total bets placed at their location. Maceos were also involved in bingo, payout pinball machines, tip books, policy tickets, punch boards, as well as many other non-gambling operations such as food and beverage sales.

There is an account that Sam Maceo began to build a twenty-unit apartment at Snug Harbor on 23rd and Avenue Q for the high rollers to use when they came down to the island to gamble. There was a meeting, behind closed doors, between Rose Maceo and W. L. Moody Jr. where Moody was reported to have said, "I have stayed out of the gambling business, I expect you to stay out of the hotel business." The building was razed in mid construction.

Sam was indicted for drug trafficking in 1937. He posted a $10,000 bond. After fighting extradition, he stood trial in New York five years later. When exonerated of the charge, he put his head in his hands and wept openly in the court room. There has never been any evidence to prove that the Maceos had ever been involved with drugs. The drugs found in Sam's car were said to have been planted there by a local prostitute. The Maceos had done a lot of good things for the children, the people, and the City Galveston. Dealing in narcotics would have destroyed their reputation and could have well

FEC # 6 L To R: Jay-r, Eddie, Sedgie, and Sam Maceo at Fat Stock Show with purchase for Turf Grill. Steer owner was Anthony Menotti of Dickinson. Galveston Isle Magazine. March, 1948.

led to their demise.

It is my firm belief that the strength of the Maceo organization kept organized crime, that was running rampant in the rest of the country, out of Galveston. Members of Al Capone's Chicago mob and Albert Anastasia's New York underworld were among the visitors to Galveston that were ask to leave and encouraged not to return. The Maceos may have made money from illegal gambling and liquor sales, but no one was forced to partake in these vices. The money that was made on the island, stayed on the island, except for Sam's suits. Sam always dressed to the nines. He had all of his suits tailor made in New York City. It is common knowledge that the Maceos were superb people to work for. They gave large amounts of money to the church and if the community chest fell below its goal, they would visit the island businesses for more contributions or they would contribute more of their own money until the goal was met. They supported the Oleander Bowl football game, promoted the Miss Universe Pageant in Galveston, help start Splash Day, and put on free public concerts on the beach at Murdoch's Pier with top stars like Phil Harris and Frankie Laine.

FEC # 7 Frankie Laine at free beach concert. Galveston Isle Magazine, September, 1950.

The beach area had a carnival-like atmosphere. There was a Kentucky Derby merry-go-round with full size quarter horses that would actually race. The first place winner would get a free ride. The merry-go-round was one of three made. One went to Berlin and the other one was in San Francisco. When the metal frame on the merry-go-round became so rusted, from the salty sea mist, it had to be dismantled, the wooden horses were stored in the defunct Hollywood Dinner Club. They were lost to the world when the Hollywood burned on August 13, 1959. There was also a Ferris wheel, a large roller-coaster and a game of chance called Corno, that paid out money. Maceos brought professional boxing and world champion pool tournaments to the Turf Athletic Club. The Maceo

FEC # 8 Old post card, postdated April 24, 1955.

organization bought all of the supplies it could, from island merchants. For merchandise they couldn't find on the island, they sometimes would open a shop, employing island residents, and produce the items they needed. It has been reported that they employed up to 2,500 people, or 10% of the adult population of Galveston.

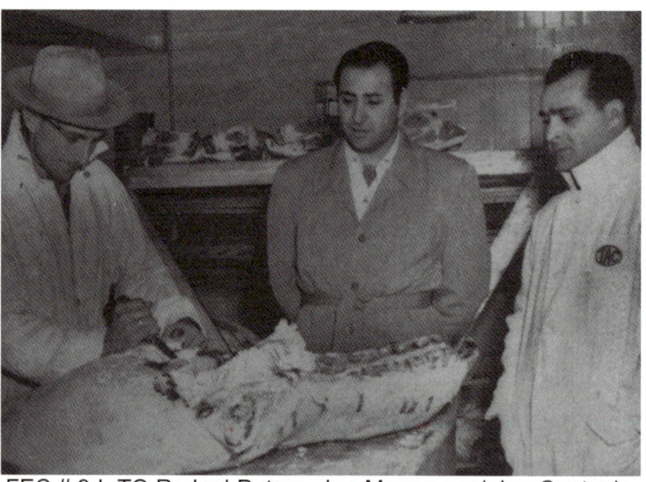
FEC # 9 L TO R: Joel Peters, Joe Maceo, and Joe Centenio with prized beef from Houston Fat Stock Show being served in the Turf Grill. Galveston Isle Magazine. March, 1950.

Reported crime was down on the island. Many credited this fact to Maceo's own private patrol, "Rose's Night Riders." Their duty was to watch over the slot machine business and preserve harmony in their clubs. The Night Riders were credited twice with saving the life of Federal Agent Al Scharff when hired guns were sent to assassinate him. They said, “One Al Scharff alive is less trouble than the fifty that would be sent to replace him if he were murdered.” Galveston, like the rest of the nation had segregation, but the Jim Crow laws were rarely enforced unless there were complaints. The only thing that was of real concern to the police was miscegenation.

There was at least one large marijuana haul in the late 1930's by an unnamed group. Marijuana was legal in the United States prior to 1936. Anyone could walk into a drugstore and buy a three inch by six inch bale of the herb. They would boil it in water, drain off the liquid, reheat it, dip a towel in the liquid and apply it to any part of their body that was plagued with rheumatism. Galvestonians could also purchase a product called “Jamaica Ginger,” also known as “Jake.” People who drank it would limp around town and were regarded as cripples. Their affliction became known as “Jake Leg.” It is now known that Jake users went to dangerous lengths to get high. Not unlike some of the drugs that are taken today. Why do you think it's called dope? “Don't do drugs,” “Just say NO!”

I ran into Dale Roberts, CEO of the Communicators Federal Credit Union in Houston, at the Astohall indoor trade market recently, where he related this anecdote to me about his brother, Edward Lee Roberts. Edward had a delivery route with the Carnation Milk Company in Galveston, where he delivered dairy products to both residential and business customers. Ed's dairy route included the Sam Maceo's home, in the Cedar Lawn subdivision. The Maceos also wanted Coca-Cola delivered to their home, but due to their strong concern for security, they wouldn't let just anyone make deliveries in or around their home. With the influence, only the Maceos had on the island, they coerced the Coca-Cola Company into hiring Ed, pay him twice what he was making with Carnation, and give him a Coca-Cola delivery route that included their home.

Dale's brother told him the Maceo home was like a fortress. There were men armed with Thompson submachine guns around the house. Ed had earned the Maceo's trust while he was with Carnation, consequently he could come and go with just a nod of the head.

At 8:10 A. M. on April 16, 1947, a ship was docked at the petrochemical complex in the Texas City Port. Its cargo was highly volatile ammonium nitrate fertilizer. The same type of ammonium nitrate fertilizer that was mixed with fuel oil to make the 4,800 pound bomb that was used in the April 19, 1995 Oklahoma City bombing of the Alfred P. Murrah Federal Building, which killed 168 and injured 800, when it caught fire and exploded at 9:12 A. M. Twenty-seven members of the Texas City Volunteer Fire Department were feverishly fighting the fires. The ship's captain had ordered the fire-smothering steam system activated to keep the cargo from being damaged by water hoses, but this act produced a combustible gas. What happened next became known as the "Texas City Disaster." The French cargo ship, SS *Grandcamp,* exploded, instantly killing all of the Texas City Firemen. The explosion sent thousands of tons of steel flying through the air, knocking two airplanes out of the sky like shot Mallards. It ignited fires on the docks, and set fuel storage tanks ablaze. The devastation was unbelievable. Mutilated human bodies were scattered everywhere and fires burned out of control. Six-teen hours later another ship, the *High Flyer* exploded, flinging its four-ton turbine engine, four thousand feet across the bay. The blasts claimed 581 lives, injured 3,500, and $100 million in damage.

Sam immediately recognized an immense need for help. He called his friend Phil Harris in Hollywood, California to help him set up a troupe of stellar entertainers to hold a relief benefit to raise money for the victims of the Texas City Disaster. The benefit was held at the Galveston City Auditorium. Everyone attending the benefit paid admission, be it one of the workers, firemen, police, or politician, they all paid. Some of the stars that donated their talents were Frank Sinatra, Jack Benny, Gene Autry, Marjorie Reynolds,

FEC # 10 L TO R: Marjorie Reynolds, screen star. Ed Buyd, Bee Walton, Bill Kraft, Mrs. and Mr. Sam Maceo at Balinese Room. Courtesy of Rosenberg Library, Galveston, Texas.

Phil Silvers, Phil Harris, George Burns and Gracie Allen, Kay Keyser, Jane Russell, Victor Borge, Alice Faye, Diana Lynn, Celeste Holm, and Bob Hope. It's a little known fact that Sam also held a private benefit at the Balinese Room, at $1000 a head, with all of the stars that had performed at the auditorium and contributed the entire proceeds to victims of the disaster.

Maceos had gambling equipment in every small town in Galveston area. In 1949 they came upon the wrath of the Reverend Harry Burch of La Marque. His sermons were filled with lectures warning of the sins of gambling. He had the backing of his congregation and almost every citizen in the town. Three of Maceo's men went to see Reverend Burch and even offered to make a cash contribution to him or his church, but it was all for nil. "All I want are those nickel-gulping monsters out of our town," replied Burch. Sam made a personal visit La Marque to talk with the Reverend. It's unknown what transpired at the meeting, but Sam directed his men take the machines out of La Marque and to keep them out. Besides, Sam knew it was just a hop, skip, and a jump, between La Marque and Galveston.

Sam Maceo died April 16, 1951 of cancer at Johns Hopkins Hospital. Following Sam's death, Rose took over all aspects of the operations. Rose died March 15, 1954 of heart failure. After Sam and Rose went to run the casinos in the clouds, the organization was run by their nephews, Anthony J. Fertitta and Victor J. Fertitta. There were many other Maceo and Fertitta family members involved in the business, but Anthony and Victor held the reins. Compared to Sam and Rose, it was a short ride.

FEC # 11 L TO R: Mrs. Frank Maceo and Vic Maceo, Mrs. and Mr. Anthony Fertitta, Mrs. and Mr. Rose Maceo. Galveston Isle Magazine. March, 1948.

In 1951 the Internal Revenue Service applied pressure on the operators by requiring them to purchase a $50 federal gambling permits. In 1957 Galveston possessed 258 permits, Corpus Christi had 145, and Jefferson County, (Beaumont and Port Author) came in third with 77. There were also state and local licenses, "taxes" on each machine. The IRS filed an income tax evasion suit against the estate of Sam Maceo and his family members. They won a $600,000 judgment in 1964. Sam Serio, the Maceo's accountant, told of Rose Maceo bringing a small safe into the Turf Grill Building, opening it and saying to his brother Sam. "Here's $600,000, three hundred of it is yours and three hundred is mine and none for the IRS." The safe nor it's content ever showed up on the books or in the estate inventory.

On June 8, 1951, State Attorney General Price Daniel, secured a district court injunction prohibiting Southwestern Bell Telephone Company from allowing the use of its phone lines to transmit horse racing information from other states to the Turf Athletic Club and four other Maceo bookie joints. To elude this new regulation, the Maceos arranged for a bar owner in Orange, Texas to accumulate all of the race results in Louisiana, scoot back across the Texas state line, posthaste, and phone the information to a Maceo bookie stationed at a phone booth near the Turf Athletic Club.

Price Daniel closed five Maceo clubs and other Galveston County gambling joints and bordellos on June 17, 1951. Many claimed it was a political move to get himself elected governor in 1952. After a brief hiatus, most of the larger clubs reopened.

A 1951 Galveston grand jury returned twenty-two felony indictments against the Maceo organization. The trials were postponed five times by the judges and finally dismissed by the county attorney for lack of evidence. The slot machines were returned in 1954. The 1956 grand jury reported that it was common knowledge that there was, "Open gambling, illegal sale of liquor, the sale of intoxicants to minors, and prostitution in Galveston County," but there were no charges presented to the grand jury by the law enforcement officers. There were many attempts to close down Galveston. The state crime investigation committee was one of them. They just couldn't get convictions by Galveston juries on felony charges. It may have been that the juries wouldn't convict them, not out of fear, but out of respect.

The Texas Rangers made innumerable raids and had seized money and property. Texas law stated that all confiscated money and equipment must be used by some state subsidiary. Many government offices got equipped with fancy leather chairs, fans, desks, and air conditioners. Raided gamblers signed a legal waver permitting the destruction of seized funds and property. In almost 100% of the cases, "We have never been sued for the return of anything," Ranger Captain Hardy Purvis said. "Last week, we found we had so many gambling chips and dice that we had to send a truck load out to an incinerator," the Captain added. "*OUCH!*"

Will Wilson ran for state attorney general in 1956 and won. He took office in January 1957 and said, "I will wait until spring, to see if the local officials will do anything to clean up Galveston." In February 1957, the newly elected Sheriff, Paul Hopkins, raided a club in Kemah, confiscating some liquor and gambling equipment. Wilson had sixty Texas Rangers ready to raid the gambling spots and held a secret meeting in Houston with twenty-three assistant lawyers. Before the raids could take place, the gambling joints in five counties mysteriously started to close, including the Balinese Room. There had been a leak.

Bill Kugle, who had been a paratrooper during WW II and fought the Japanese in the Pacific, was a young state legislator from Galveston in 1953. He was in the State Capitol coffee shop one night talking to two for his associates, "Barefoot" Sanders and Don Kennard, and mentioned that, "Galveston was in a sad state of affairs and an insult to every law-abiding citizen of Texas." He was overheard by Ralph Dodd, a reporter for the Houston Press, and asked if he could be quoted. Kugle said that it would be fine with him. The next day's headline read, "Galveston Official Raps Gambling." Kugle received several phone calls concerning him and his family's health and well being. He was later offered a $30,000 cash retainer, for future services, by the late Representative Harold Seay. Kugle refused to compromise and turned it down. He confided with his law-school friend and former FBI agent, James P. Simpson, from Texas City, about the offer. Simpson told Kugle that he had learned about the bribe attempt from a local FBI agent. Mr. Simpson told me in an interview. "I knew damn well he wouldn't take it. Kugle was an impeccably honest man." Another friend, Jim Bradner, owner of a Galveston radio station, arranged to plant a bug in Kugle's office.

A short time later, the owner of five pelvic palaces in Galveston, Sam Amelio, requested an appointment with Kugle. He offered Kugle a $1,500 payoff. "Is that what you pay the police commissioner?" Kugle asked. "Yes, I'm going to pay you the same amount I pay Walter Johnston." Kugle again refused the money and took the tape to the grand jury. Amelio was subpoenaed for the attempted bribe a state legislator. He denied the meeting with Kugle and was indicted for perjury. There wasn't enough evidence to indict Johnston, but at least the tape would be heard when Amelio had his day in court. Before he could spill the beans at his trial, Amelio "fall down and go boom" in one of his houses of ill repute. His body was found at the bottom of the stairs with $2,500 in traveler's checks and a baseball sized knot on the back of his head. In 1954 Kugle ran for office again, but the forces against him were to strong. He carried the mainland, failed to the needed votes in Galveston. His political career over, he moved his family off the island.

In the same election, James P. Simpson ran for county attorney, but lost by eight votes. He planned on running for office again in 1956, but decided to open his law practice instead of battling the pro-gambling forces in Galveston at the polls. Simpson had a personal vendetta against the rackets in Galveston and was bound and determined to clean up the island. He found his chance when Will Wilson was elected attorney general of Texas. Wilson had cleaned up the Dallas area while he was its county attorney. Wilson had not yet been sworn in, when Simpson penned him a letter, explaining how he wanted to rid Galveston of its vices and how they could accomplish it. Simpson had learned from his experience with the FBI, that you had to plant someone on the inside to get the evidence that would stand up in court. Wilson had discovered, while a county attorney in Dallas, the use of undercover agents to secure evidence.

FEC # 12 James P. Simpson in a 1997 photograph standing in front of a display of his WW II mementos at his office in Texas City. The display was made by Mrs. Simpson.

Wilson had an eye on the governor's office. If he could clean up Galveston, with Simpson's help, it wouldn't be just a feather in his hat, in could be a full headdress. This of course, was not the sole reason Wilson wanted to rid Galveston of the rackets. Wilson was a WW II hero in the Pacific, a very courageous man, and he believed the laws should be enforced and that nobody should be above the law. Wilson appointed James P. Simpson special assistant and gave him carte blanche to acquire the hard evidence needed to close down the rackets.

Jim Simpson, himself a WW II hero, having flown sixty combat missions over Nazi Germany, was not afraid of the pro-gambling forces. If any harm had come to a young married man with a child, who had bought a home and planted roots in the county, it would be the end. Not even their friends in high places could not protect them. Some may have thought Simpson was still with the FBI, sent here by J. Edgar Hoover, as an undercover agent. Jim Simpson was the attorney for the Oil, Chemical, and Atomic Workers International Union. He enlisted two oil company workers for the undercover operations. They were James D. "Bubby" Givens, thirty-three, of 2207 Scott, La Marque, an employee of Republic Oil and Refining Company, and Carroll S. Yaws, thirty-seven, of Alta Loma, an employee of American Oil Company. Givens was chairman of the Galveston County Democratic Executive Committee. Simpson gave them a crash course on compiling evidence and record keeping. Working together, the pair went to various establishments, buying drinks, playing slot machines, blackjack and dice, or talking to the ladies in the bawdy houses. They continued working their regular day jobs at the refineries and worked at their dangerous, exhausting assignments at night. Starting at approximately 8:00 P. M. and ending around 2:00 A. M. and sometimes a lot later. Their investigation continued over a four month period and consisted of about thirty nights work.

Givens and Yaws had set their cross hairs on the Maceo empire. To achieve this task, they had to become well known at the Turf Athletic Club's Western Room. Once this was accomplished, they could gain admittance to the Balinese Room. After a few visits, they made friends with the receptionist at the Western Room. They told her it was Yaw's birthday and Given's wedding anniversary, which it really was, and that they wanted to take their wives to the Balinese Room for dinner. The receptionist made a phone call.

Bingo, they were in. It was on April 29, they make their first visit to the Balinese Room. Once admitted, they ordered drinks, saw three dice tables, two roulette wheels, six slot machines, a race horse machine, and a gaming room. Givens placed bets at the roulette wheel and lost $10, then went to the dice table and won some money. He ended up breaking even when the night was over. They returned to the Balinese Room on May 3, 17, & 24. Givens and Yaws gathered evidence on about fifty clubs and bawdy houses in Galveston area with their painstaking work.

On one of their undercover investigations in Kemah, they were asked by a local bartender if they would like to get in on a large game. They said, "Yes." They got into their car and followed the bartender down a dark, desolate, road to a waterfront club. Their car was valet parked, but they had forgotten their notebook in the car's unlocked glove compartment. The book contained detailed listings of dates, places, and all the evidence of their undercover work. If the book had been found while they were inside gambling, they were confident they would be sleeping with the fishes. They hurriedly placed a few large bets and left. Their luck had held out, the real purpose for being there went undiscovered.

The undercover work was an enormous success, they had all the evidence they needed. Wednesday, June 5, 1957, was the day it started to rain on Maceo's parade. In the afternoon on the day of the raid, two attorney generals arrived on the island to secure the search warrants they needed from a District Judge Donald M. Markle, a rock of honor that could be trusted to keep it a secret. The other District Judge William E. Stone, was also a man who was above reproach. Undercover agents from the Texas Department of Public Safety began infiltrating the clubs just after dark. The cadre of lawmen, sixty Texas Rangers, twenty-three assistant attorneys and other Department of Public Safety officers met in the auditorium of the Junior League building in Houston. They were divided into five units. Each unit had a few Texas Rangers, an assistant attorney, and a larger squad DPS troopers. Price Daniel was Governor and Wilson had his full support. Raids were planned for Harris, Fort Bend, Jefferson, and Brazoria Counties, but the main concentration was to be in Galveston County.

The plan was to leave for Galveston, from Houston at 11:30 P. M. There were over one-hundred lawmen involved in this history making raid. The phone rang at the Houston assembling location and the Chief Ranger, Homer Garrison said, "Boys, somebody tipped them off. They didn't open tonight and all the gambling equipment has mysteriously vanished." The biggest raid in Texas history, never took place. As far as I know it has never been determined who let the cat out of the bag. The gambling operators in Galveston knew that Will Wilson was dead serious and as Jim Simpson expressed. "They knew there wasn't enough gold in Fort Knox to buy Will Wilson." They had survived numerous forays in the past, of course

FEC # 13 L To R: James C. Broode Sr., Police Chief Willie Burns smashing H. C. Evans' Bang Tails Winter Book horse race machine, and Jean Hasey. September, 1949. Courtesy of Rosenberg Library, Galveston, Texas.

they knew well in advance when and where many of them were going to take place.

FEC # 14-A OBV. H. C. Evans Bang Tails. Courtesy Vern Blanck.

FEC # 14-B REV. H. C. Evans Winter Book. Courtesy Vern Blanck.

On Monday, June 10, ten of Wilson's assistants began filling suits seeking restraining orders and injunctions against forty-seven gambling, prostitution houses, and night spots in Galveston County. This maneuver was an enormous surprise to the operators of these clubs. It left them helpless. There was no way to get around the temporary and permanent injunctions.

Armed with a fist full of search warrants, Jim Simpson, a squad of Rangers, the assistant attorney general, went to every location on the attorney general's list. The Rangers smashed marble, horse race, and slot machines, confiscated betting records, and seized everything they could find that even looked like it had anything to do with gambling. The Texas Department of Public Safety Troopers seized gambling equipment on the causeway as it was being rushed off the island. The raiders knew they wouldn't find any gambling equipment in the Balinese Room nor in any of the other Maceo clubs. The attorney general had a small office with a phone set up on the island by this time. A snitch called Simpson and told him where to look, in the defunct Hollywood Dinner Club.

FEC # 15 Unidentified Galveston lawman destroying slots in 1949 raid.

The Hollywood Dinner Club and the Turf Club were raided and wrecked by ax wheeling Texas Rangers in 1939. Orders for that raid came from the newly elected governor, James V. Allred. With a several new slot machines, the Turf Club reopened, but the Hollywood would never open again. A court injunction closed it permanently after some narcotics were found on one of the patrons. It was turned into a Maceo warehouse. Angelo Montalbano, an employee of the Turf Athletic Club, told me in an interview, that the man who was in charge of the HDC called him and asked if he would take a ride with him. Angelo said, "Sure." He didn't tell him where they were going, but unfortunately, they were going to the Hollywood Dinner Club. The attorney general's office had call and said they wanted to meet him out there. They wanted to go in. Both men went into the building with Simpson and the Rangers. The place was jam packed with slot machines, some of them brand new, still in their shipping crates. There were Winter Book horse race machines, roulette wheels, and gaming tables. Angelo remembered that the Rangers weren't angry, in fact they were very friendly. The Rangers said they would meet them there in the morning. The next morning, June 19, 1957, the Rangers had their eighteen wheelers backed up to the building. They unlocked the doors and the Rangers loaded up all the gambling equipment. The Rangers confiscated fifteen hundred slots, of which twelve hundred were electric models, and some were beautiful console models. Also seized were roulette wheels, card and dice tables, and cases of dice and chips. The $100 chips, inscribed "Balinese Room," indicated they had discovered the cache of at least part of the gambling equipment that had so quickly disappeared from the Balinese Room, just before the scheduled raids, that never occurred. Some of the confiscated slots were stored by the Rangers in a bonded warehouse owned by Wiley and Nicholls Co. Inc. in Galveston.

Also found, in three warehouses and an underground bunker, at old Fort Travis on Bolivar Peninsula, were about five hundred slot and marble machines, along with other gambling equipment. All were the old one-armed-bandit type. Some were still in their shipping crates. Others were found to have the jackpot channels plugged with rags. This would indicate that even if a player lined up three jackpots on the reels, the machine wouldn't payoff. I find this very hard to believe. It doesn't take a rocket scientist to figure out that if you line up three jackpots and it doesn't payoff something is terribly wrong. Either the machine is broken or you are being cheated. Whichever the case, you would demand your money. If they refused to pay, word would soon get out that they were running a crooked club and they would soon go out of business or they might have an unexplained fire. If they wanted to rig the machines, they could have used a percentage clip for the star wheel. This device prevents the reels from stopping on a jackpot. It fits inside the machine where no one could see it. The clips cost $1 each or $9 a dozen. Without a working knowledge of slot machines, they believed the rags stopped it for paying out a jackpot, but I think this is what they found. As the

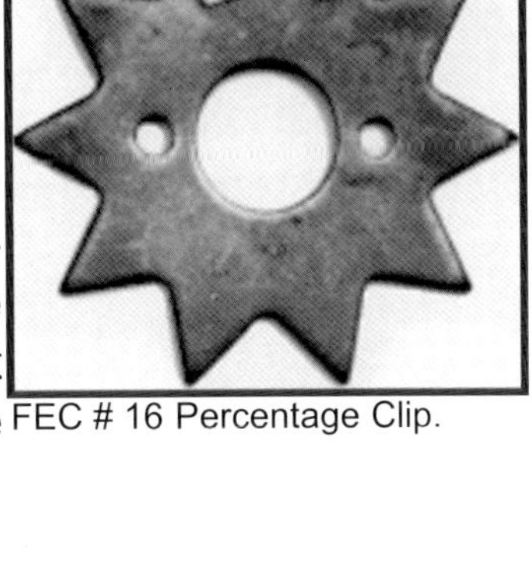

FEC # 16 Percentage Clip.

handle on the machine is pulled, the coins fall into a vertical payout tube, to be used on later payouts. When this tube gets full, the coins fall into the reserve jackpot hopper and then into the jackpot hopper. This action keeps the hoppers full. If the coins piled up in the jackpot hoppers it could add $10 or more to the jackpot payout. After the jackpot hoppers are full, the coins fall into the cash box, that is emptied by the operators. I think the rags may have been stuffed into the top of the jackpot hoppers so that only the amount of money the operator put in the jackpot would be paid out, thus they could regulate how much money was payed out when someone hit a jackpot. I have a second theory. The machines were found in the old abandon gun bunkers and were covered with dust. This meant they had been there for quite a while and may have remained hidden there for some time to come. The rags could have been stuffed in the bottom of the jackpot channels to prevent rattlesnakes, mice, and other varmints from making a home in the machines. The jackpot channels are generally the only access opening to the inside of a slot machine.

An acquaintance of mine, and a fellow depression glass dealer, Steve Dowell of Austin, Texas, shared this story with me on my last trip to his fine city. He grew up in Houston and was in high school in 1959. Steve and two of his friends were rummaging around on Bolivar Peninsula one day and discovered an old warehouse. Upon exploring it they found a cache of gambling paraphernalia and slot machines that had been hidden from the raiding Rangers.

They decided to take a few of the slot machines home and have some fun. This was just a couple of years after the much publicized raids in Galveston by the Texas Rangers, so it was fresh on everyone's mind. Any account of gambling made good news stories. Steve said they would take one of the machines, toss it in a ditch, call the authorities, give them the skinny on its location, then sit back and watch what happened.

There were stories flying around about how the machines may have fallen of the back of a truck and the speculation of organized crime moving into the area. Houston had its share of illegal gambling places, they were just not as open about it as they were in Galveston. They did this every few weeks for a couple of months before they decided that they had better quit before they got caught. In those days it was illegal to own a slot machine or any parts for one. Today after two changes in the laws it is now legal to own any vintage video or slot machine as long as it is for use at a private place.

One of the friends has since passed away, the other one is still living in Houston. Steve said he was sure he wouldn't want his name published.

The Rangers found another three-hundred slot machines in a warehouse at Forty-sixth Street and Gore in Dickinson. The cache was reported to be from the estate of the late Joe Jiambo who owned the Rose Garden. Phillip Barberia, was the current owner of the Rose Garden and Jiambo's nephew, was reportedly in charge of the warehouse, signed the destruction order at the scene. Rangers put the machines out of operation with their sledge hammers, then hauled them to the dump. Retrieved from the dump, with the permission from the Rangers, the machines were sold as scrap metal by the Dickinson Little League and the motors from the electric models were used by the Dickinson Optimist Radio Club.

The Rangers smashed a wide variety of gambling paraphernalia. It would have wrecked the Rangers if they had tried to demolish that much equipment with their ten pound sledge hammers. Wilson flew to Houston after hearing about the fifteen hundred slot machines being found the night before behind some musty draperies at the Hollywood Dinner Club. He toured the Hollywood, then went to watch the $1,000,000 bonfire at the city dump that had been ignited by Texas Ranger Captain Johnny Klevenhagen and Sergeant Pete Rogers. The large blaze was extinguished at midnight because the fire marshal went off duty and the fire tenders had reached a mass of cast-iron slots that wouldn't burn.

Simpson was told by Bob Bray, a reporter for the Houston Chronicle and a stringer for *Life Magazine,* that if he could stage a public display of the disposal of the confiscated equipment, he could arrange to have *Life Magazin*e to send a reporter to photograph it. Simpson thought he came up with the perfect plan. They would load the contraband on a barge and dump it into Galveston Bay. But not just anywhere in the bay, he would use a Galveston landmark, the *SS Selma* as a backdrop. The *SS Selma* was one of thirteen reinforced concrete steam tankers that was built to save steel during WW I. She was launched June 28, 1919, in Mobile, Alabama, the same day the war ended. She was used to transport oil between the United States and Mexico for a while, before hitting a jetty off

Tampico, Mexico. The damaged *SS Selma* was towed to Galveston for repairs. No one could be found to do the repairs, so she was scuttled in 1922 and rests peacefully, partially submerged in the flats, just east of Pelican Island in Galveston Bay. If you ever get to Galveston, be sure to take the free ferry to Bolivar Peninsula, look to the north where you can see her resting in the tranquil blue waters of Galveston Bay. She can also be seen from Seawolf Park

FEC # 17 Courtesy of A. Pat Daniels. The *SS Selma* at rest, in Galveston Bay.

on Pelican Island. There have been at least five owners since she went to her watery grave. One owner was going to build a fishing facility but that never transpired. There were rumors of a Nazi spy hiding in the ship and track shipping movements in the Galveston ship channel during World War II. Ten days after Nazi Germany declared war on the United States, they sent five Type-9 U-Boats, to attack shipping on the East Coast of North America and in the Gulf on Mexico. The British had intercepted their radio transmissions and reported it to the U.S. Navy, but nothing or little was done about it. The first strike date was January 13, with twenty-five ships being sunk on that day. The subs sank a total of almost 400 ships that claimed close to 5,000 lives. Almost 50% of the U.S. oil supply was coming from Houston, Texas City, and Galveston refineries and was being shipped through the Galveston Bay Ship Channel, directly passed the SS Selma. There were newspaper reports of five or six ships being sunk, then the reports stopped. In the almost two years the subs were in the Gulf of Mexico, they sank fifty-six ships and damaged another fourteen.

I am fortunate to be invited to the *SS Selma's* annual birthday party given by her new owners, Shirley and A. Pat Daniels. Through the diligent efforts of Mr. Daniels, the *SS Selma* has been recognized as a Recorded Texas Historic Landmark by the Texas Historical Commission and has been entered in the National Register of Historic Places by the National Park Service. This is in addition to its recognition earlier as a State Archeological Landmark by the Texas Antiquities Committee and as the official flagship of The Texas Army. In 1964 her sale price was $750, which is about what its worth today on the Galveston County's tax roll. Pat purchased her for an undisclosed amount in 1992.

Wilson, his men, and Simpson, gathered at Pier 18 where they loaded some fifty slots on two pilot boats of the Coastwise Pilot and Boat Service. When they arrived in the vicinity of the *SS Selma* in Galveston Bay, the slots were pushed overboard in about thirty-five feet of water, but *Life Magazine* was no where to be found. Could it have been the result of the August 5, 1955, alleged attack of Hank Suydam and Joe Scherschel, two *Life* staff reporters, by Anthony J. Fertitta and two of his henchmen, after the reporters were seen taking photographs of the Turf Grill Building, that kept the magazine away? Mayor George Clough and Major T. Charles Mewshaw, commander the Army Corps of Engineers, immediately accused Wilson, Simpson, and company of illegal dumping refuse without a permit and creating a hazard to navigation in Galveston Bay. When Wilson was asked what he would do if the Corps of Engineers ordered him to "fish them up," he replied, "I can't swim that deep." Many stories surfaced about the fish with three fruit eyes floating around the ship channel but they just weren't true. I'm a dealer in antique slot machines and they weight an average of about seventy-five pounds. The only wood is on the bottom and two sides. Some have no wood at all on them. Simpson said, the machines sank like rocks, the console models may have taken a few minutes to sink, but they sank. There were reports of shrimpers pulling up slot machines in their shrimp nets. In a statement a few days later the Corps of Engineers said they couldn't find any floating slot machines and soundings made by the Engineers indicated the slots came to rest close to the edge of the *SS Selma* and presented no navigational hazard.

Even after the accomplishment after closing down the gambling in Galveston, Wilson lost the race for governor. Maybe more voters than he contemplated were pro-gambling? He more or less retired form public life because of the Sharpstown banking scandal. Jim Simpson believes that Will Wilson was not guilty of any wrong doing and that anybody that was within a ten-mile radius of Frank Sharp became tainted. Guilty or not, the gambling supporters on the island smiled when they spoke of the banking scandal.

Anthony J. Fertitta came to trial in 1959 on charges of permitting gambling in the Balinese Room. He was found guilty and received a two year suspended sentence. Anthony went to Las Vegas for a short time, moved back to Houston and worked at Glenn McCarthy's Cork Club in the Shamrock Hotel. He ended up in his hometown of Leesville, Louisiana, where, with his brother Sam, they entered into the home construction business and he was later elected mayor. Victor J. Fertitta died in 1960 before he could be brought to trial. There were a few other trials, but the majority of the indictments were never pursed. The courts dropped one-hundred and sixty-four cases in 1969.

After the closing of Galveston's casinos, many of the operators and employees went into legitimate businesses. Bert Nickels, manager of the Texas Employment Commission reported an increase in application for jobs. Nickels stated that the figures were confidential, but United Press reported more than fifty former gamblers and barmen had applied for work. Some relocated to Arkansas and others went to neighboring Texas cities to ply the trades they had learned working in the gambling clubs in Galveston. Many went to Las Vegas, where some can still be found today.

Gangster Benjamin "Bugsy" Siegel went to Vegas in the summer of 1941 to run the wire service for the mob for the just legalized horse race betting. Gambling had become legal again in Nevada in 1931. The gambling casinos downtown were not much more than small bars with sawdust and peanut shell covered floors. Contrary to the news media and the flicks, Bugsy didn't drive seven miles out the strip, walk into the desert, kick some sand, and say. "This is where I will build the Flamingo." The El Rancho, four miles out on the strip, was up and running when Bugsy first arrived in town and the Last Frontier opened in 1942. Billy Wilkerson, a restaurateur from Los Angeles, started the Flamingo but ran out of financing. Bugsy became a partner, invested the mob's funds, and eventually squeezed Wilkerson out. The rest of the legend has been reported pretty much more or less the way it happened. The Flamingo opened on December 26, 1946 as Bugsy had promised Weyer Lansky and Lucky Luciano, but the thirty plus star entertainers billed for opening had to stay at the VIP rooms at the El Rancho. The Flamingo closed on February 1, 1947, while construction of the two-hundred hotel rooms was completed. It reopened March 1, 1947, and was starting to show a profit but it was too slow for Lansky and Luciano. Bugsy died of lead poisoning in Virginia Hill's Beverly Hills mansion at 10:30 P. M. June 20, 1947.

Galveston's gambling business had started to decline in the 50's. More people were going to Las Vegas. Unlike Galveston, Vegas has large fancy hotels with a casino in them. You could sleep, eat, be entertained, and gamble without going out in the weather. There were a wider variety of games that could be played and best of all it was legal. If gambling had been legal in Galveston, Vegas may not have become what it is today. Vegas learned how to do what it does from the Maceos. Good food, stellar entertainers, first class service, personal safety, and honest games of chance. Galveston has an overall better year round climate, short of an occasional hurricane for excitement. It's located in the center of the country, has deep-sea fishing and an ocean just a few feet away.

Galveston voters have turned down a non-binding referendum on gambling in 1984, 1987, and 1988. A bill to allow casino style gambling was in the state legislature in 1995. It was to be voted on, but it never came up for a vote due to an opinion written by the state attorney general. I believe it is just a matter of time before we have legalized casino gambling in the state. You can again gamble in Galveston, this time legally, on our full-blown state lottery. La Marque, in Galveston County, has the beautiful Gulf Greyhound Park dog racing track. Houston sports the Sam Houston Race Park horse racing facility. There are other horse tracks around the state with more being built. Galveston saw it's first gambling cruise ship in 1989, *The Pride of Galveston,* formally the *Pride of Mississippi,* that was promptly joined by *The Star of Texas.* Both ships have both long since sailed off in the sunset, never to return.

FEC # 18 OBV. & REV.
Pride of Galveston.

FEC # 19 OBV. & Rev.
Star of Texas.

Texas has two Indian Reservation casinos. El Paso has the Speaking Rock Casino. The Seven Circle Resorts wasn't on the reservation land and was never opened.

FEC # 20-A OBV.
Speaking Rock.

FEC # 20-B REV.
Seven Circle.

Eagle Pass possesses the Kickapoo, Lucky Eagle Casino.

FEC # 21-A OBV.
Lucky Eagle.

FEC # 21-B REV.
Lucky Eagle.

Many of our tax dollars are boarding jets and flying off to Las Vegas, Reno, Atlantic City, and hundreds of other cities. There are free buses leaving Houston every day, taking gamblers and their money to the casinos just across the Louisiana state line.

In late 1995, Tilman Fertitta purchased the old Key Largo Resort Hotel, the San Luis Hotel, and has developed a resort and conference center on the twenty-two acres that surrounds the hotels on the Seawall Boulevard. In early 1997 he has also purchased the six restaurants on the Kemah waterfront, making him the sole owner of all the eateries on Galveston Bay and the Clear Lake yacht channel. Kemah is on south side of the yacht channel in Galveston County. Seabrook in on the north side of the yacht channel in Harris County. Galveston is a natural for gambling. One day it may again be known as, *Galveston Island of Chance.*

About the Establishments

Not all of the establishments listed on the forthcoming pages had open gambling. Some were private clubs, which were not open to the general public. Most of these clubs had some type of gambling for their members. There were many other clubs that I have not listed, that I'm sure had gambling. I have tried to list clubs that I had proof, or a very strong suspicion of having some type of gambling. Some were only open for a very short period of time, perhaps a few months or weeks. Not all of the clubs had gambling chips and some of the ones that did, had the club owner's initials on them. Some of the chip manufactures would make chips with the club owner's initials on them. They were given to the club owners for their personal home use. These are referred to as "personalized" chips.

The numerical Streets in Galveston run North and South and the alphabetical Avenues run East and West. The streets and avenues also have names. Some of the addresses of the clubs are listed numerically or alphabetically and some by street name. Seawall Boulevard was just called Boulevard. The following list may help clear up some of this confusion.

Ave. A ------------ Water
Ave. B ------------ The Strand
Ave. C ------------ Mechanic
Ave. D ------------ Market
Ave. E ------------ Postoffice
Ave. F ------------ Church
Ave. G ----------- Winnie
Ave. H ------------ Ball
Ave. I ------------ Sealy
Ave. J ------------ Broadway

THE ESTABLISHMENTS

ACE ROOMS

2600 Market St., Galveston, owner/operator, Jesse Elliot. Was one of the 47 night spots listed in the June 11, 1957 injunctions. Bawdy house and liquor violations.

ACME ROOMS

3713½ Market St., Galveston, owner/operator, Marie Allen and Margaret Lera. Was one of the 47 night spots listed in the June 11, 1957 injunctions. Bawdy house and liquor violations.

ADELPHI CLUB

3027 ½ Ave. M, Galveston, owner/operator, Lucius Humphrey.

ALAMO CLUB

2009 23rd St., Galveston, owner/operator, Abe T. Rosenthal and Joella W. Poole. Was one of the 47 night spots listed in the June 11, 1957 injunctions. Gambling and liquor violations. Houston Chronicle 3/2/41, "In Galveston on 3/1/41, Abe Rosenthal pleaded guilty of permitting gambling, fined $25 and court cost by Justice James A. Piperi. Charges were filed by Texas Ranger J. A. Thompson."

ALAMO CLUB

•

WHERE OLD
FRIENDS MEET

•

ABE ROSENTHAL, *Mgr.*

2009 23rd St. Phone 5221

FEC # 22 Ad from April 4, 1947. Galveston Week.

FEC # 23-A OBV. Abe T. Rosenthal.   FEC # 23-B REV. Abe T. Rosenthal.

AL'S 88 KEY

628 Seawall Boulevard, Galveston, owner/operator, Al Mason. Was one of the 47 night spots listed in the June 11, 1957 injunctions. Liquor violations.

FEC # 24 Ad from July 18, 1952.
Galveston Week.

ALTRUSA CLUB

Jean Lafitte Hotel, Galveston, owner/operator, unknown.

ANCHOR CLUB

205 20th St., Galveston, owner/operator, Lee and Ida Woodson. Was one of the 47 night spots listed in the June 11, 1957 injunctions. Gambling and liquor.

FEC # 25 OBV. & REV. Black. FEC # 26 OBV. & REV. Red. FEC # 27 OBV. & REV. Blue.

ANNEX SOCIAL CLUB

On the corner of Post Office and Tremont next-door to the Star Drug Store and the Mizpah Hotel. Owner/operator, Poppa George. The bartender's name was Jeep. The place was a late night club and had one lady-of-the-evening upstairs who's only access was behind a two-way mirror. Very few people knew of her existence, including the Maceos. The Mizpah Hotel next-door, was used as a bawdy house by the local hookers. The girls would come to the Annex, pickup a client, then return to the Mizpah where they lived.

FEC # 28 OBV. & REV. Orange.

FEC # 29 Courtesy Pinky Hull, from his book, "Is there a Leprechaun in the Gazebo?" Pinky's opening night at the Annex Social Club in 1948. 1926-1997.

ARTILLERY CLUB

1904 Seawall Blvd. One of the most pretentious clubs in Galveston. Robert Lee Fabj (Babby) had 1100 slot machines in a warehouse that belonged to the Artillery Club and the Country Club. It had the largest bawdy house on the island, immediately behind it.

BALI BALI

61st and Ave. S, Galveston, owner/operator, unknown. Note the 3:00 A. M. floor show. They had to be open for gambling.

FEC # 30 Ad from August 9/16, 1946. This Week in Galveston Note spelling of xylophonist.

DINE AND DANCE AT THE

BALI BALI

Three Floor Shows Nightly

11 P. M., 1 A. M., 3 A. M.

FEATURING

BOBBY GRAHAM, Emcee Extraordinary

BETTY REED, Zylophonist

GINGER LEE, Lovely Elimination Dancer

61st and Avenue S

PHONE 2-5569

BALINESE ROOM

2107 Seawall Blvd. at 21st St., Galveston, owners/operators, Turf Athletic Club, Gulf Properties, the Maceos, Lorainsa Grillette, Sam Serio, and the Fertittas. Was one of the 47 night spots listed in the June 11, 1957 injunctions. Gambling and liquor violations. Was previously named Chop Suey, Maceo's Grotto Dinner Club, and Sui Jen Cafe. One of the largest and most notorious clubs of the gambling era. It's one of a very few buildings that is still standing, pretty much in the same condition as it was in its heyday.

FEC # 31 Post card from Balinese Room, portraying clockwise from upper left, are the Dinning Room, Foyer, Aquarium, and Lounge. Circa 1950's. Courtesy Louis Schamerhorn.

The Balinese was nicknamed, Houston's Country Club. Some of the stellar stars that performed there were Phil Harris, Ben Bernie, Glenn Grey, Frank Sinatra, Fran Warren, Jackie Miles, Bob Cross, Roman and Martin, Ames Brothers, Three Stooges, Tony Bennett, Joe E. Lewis, Peggy Lee, Frankie Lane, Sophie Tucker, Ted Lewis, Hildegarde, Ben Blue, Nelson Eddy, Al Jolson, Eddie Cantor, Carmen Cavallaro, Chico and Harpo Marx, Jose Iturbi, and Tito Guizar. One of the Ritz Brothers had a large, long, pointed tongue, that would drive the ladies wild. Could this have been where Gene Simmons, bass player from Kiss, picked up his routine?

There was a small fire on March 8, 1953, but a larger blaze on October 3, 1953 caused the closing of the Balinese Room.

March 24, 1955

Mr. P. G. Schreiber
1709 Ave O
Galveston, Texas

Dear Mr. Schreiber:

At last we can let you in on the good news. We have decided to rebuild the Balinese Room. We anticipate construction will begin within the next sixty days and completion is expected around August 15, 1955.

With a program of this type and scope it is necessary that we prevail upon a certain group of Turf Athletic Club members to help us realize a bigger and more beautiful Balinese Room for your greater enjoyment. Our new policy will place membership on a more exclusive basis. We are happy to tell you that a screening committee has selected you to be included in this group.

It is our plan to issue Deposit Coupons amounting to not less than $100 to each selected member. Each book will provide (5) $20 coupons with the first coupon being redeemable on or after June 1st, 1956, and the remainder of coupons being honored each succeeding year of operation. These coupons are good for both food and service.

Please understand that we have embarked on this program only after talking to hundreds of Turf Athletic Club members. This Deposit Coupon plan has been most acceptable to the great majority. We feel confident it will meet with your approval, too.

If our proposal merits your consideration and acceptance you are privileged to avail yourself of this offer within thirty days from date of this letter. Because there is a limitation on both time and acceptances we urge you to act promptly. Your check for $100 should be made payable to EARL LLEWELLYN, TRUSTEE FOR TURF ATHLETIC CLUB DEPOSIT COUPON ACCOUNT and mailed to P. O. BOX 148, GALVESTON, TEXAS.

Sincerely,

Vic J. Fertitta
VICTOR J. FERTITTA

Anthony Fertitta
ANTHONY FERTITTA

VJF/jc

On the Beach · BALINESE ROOM
Telephone 2-8421
Downtown Clubrooms · STUDIO LOUNGE
Telephone 3-2311
General Offices 2214 MARKET ST., GALVESTON, TEX.

FEC # 32 Letter from the Fertittas on reopening the Balinese Room, dated March 24, 1955.

FEC # 33 Header from a 8½" x 11" hand written lunch menu.

The kitchen had a trap door in the floor that the old Chinese cook Go-Bo, who once cooked for General John J. Pershing, would fish through when things got slow. One day he hooked a enormous fish and had to be refrained from chopping the hole large enough to get the fish through. Sam didn't like him fishing on the job but when he found out the customers were amused by it, he allowed it. When the cook was found dead in his room, he had a hundred or more gallons of rice, for the hereafter, that he had pilfered, a pocket full at a time, from the kitchen.

FEC # 34 Recent photos of the Balinese Room. Courtesy Vern Blanck.

FEC # 35 Small pepper mill.

TAC

Presenting
As A Surprise Treat
Joe REICHMAN
"the Pagliacci of the Piano"
and
HIS ORCHESTRA
★
Commencing
Tuesday, August Tenth
★
Balinese Room
Galveston, Texas

FEC # 36 4¼" x 6½" invitation.

The Balinese Room had many articles that were made for and used exclusively in the club. The following are a few of these items.

FEC # 37-A Monogram on 4½" glass.

FEC # 37-B 4½" drink glass.

FEC # 38-A Matchbook, front cover.

FEC # 38-B Matchbook, inside.

FEC # 38-C Matchbook, back cover.

FEC # 39 Dinner napkin.

FEC # 40-A Matchbook, front cover. 1980's.

FEC # 40-B Matchbook, back cover.

The following box of cards must have been a gift for VIP patrons of both clubs. The box is a velveted, with the names of the Balinese Room and the Studio Lounge.

FEC # 41-A Outside of deck of cards box.

FEC # 41-B Jokers on cards.

FEC # 41-C Aces on cards.

FEC # 41-D Backs of cards.

FEC # 42 Bamboo water glass.
Courtesy Angelo Montalbano.

FEC # 43 Demitasse cup and saucer.

The following are gambling chips that were used at the Balinese Room. The only two colors known of the $500 chips.

FEC # 44 OBV. & REV.
Purple, ribbed rim.

FEC # 45 OBV. & REV.
Yellow, smooth rim.

The only two colors known of the $100 chips.

FEC # 46 OBV. & REV.
Red, ribbed rim.

FEC # 47 OBV. & REV.
Gray, smooth rim.

Even though there is no name or initials on them, these two chips are from the Balinese Room. They were given to the high rollers, so the dealers and pit bosses could recognize them. They are the only two colors known of this type of $100 chip.

FEC # 48 OBV. & REV.
Dark red, ribbed rim.

FEC # 49 OBV. & REV.
Dark purple, smooth rim.

The heart and rectangle design is believed to be the oldest of the Balinese Room chips. There may be more of the following chips, but these are all that I have seen.

FEC # 50 OBV. & REV. Tan.
Courtesy Angelo Montalbano.

FEC # 51 OBV. & REV. Red.
Courtesy Vern Blanck.

FEC # 52 OBV. & REV. Black.
Courtesy Angelo Montalbano.

The small greek key is thought to be the next oldest design used on the Balinese Room chips.

FEC # 53 OBV. & REV. Tan.
Courtesy Vern Blanck.

FEC # 54 OBV. & REV. Orange.

FEC # 55 OBV. & REV. Black.

The twenty-six diamond design is considered to be the next design used at the Balinese Room.

FEC # 56 OBV. & REV. Tan.

FEC # 57 OBV. & REV. Orange.

FEC # 58 OBV. & REV. Blue.

FEC # 59 OBV. & REV. Purple.

The next design, square in a circle, is the latest to be used at the Balinese Room.

FEC # 60 OBV. & REV. Tan.

FEC # 61 OBV. & REV. Red.

FEC # 62 OBV. & REV. Blue.

The next two chips are said to had been used at the Balinese Room. They may have been a roulette or some type of marker chip.

FEC # 63 OBV. & REV. Red.
Courtesy Vern Blanck.

FEC # 64 OBV. & REV. Red.

Sophie Tucker was scheduled to open October 12, 1953 at the Balinese Room, but instead, she lost nine trunks of costumes valued at $5000, in the big fire October 3. Sophie rescheduled and returned to a grateful audience in 1956.

Fred Astaire and Arthur Murray judged dance contests and would give free dance lessons. Entertainers that played at the Balinese Room would be payed $5,000 to $10,000 a week. In Las Vegas, they could get $100,000 a week, just for entering the building.

The Balinese Room was damaged by Hurricane Carla in 1961. It has had several owners since then and has been opened as a nightclub, extra meeting room for the nearby Galvez Hotel, hosting private parties and weddings, but none of these endeavors seemed to have made enough profit to keep open. It was last open in 1989.

Houston Rockets basketball star, Hakeem Olajuwon, was working on a deal to purchase it in 1993, but the acquisition didn't transpire, partly because of Texas Open Beaches Act, which limited the changes they wanted to make to the beachfront.

The newly formed Third Coast Preservation Inc. has formed a subsidiary called The Balinese Historical Society, a nonprofit society, to purchase and renovate the former nightclub and casino as a family-style entertainment complex with video and billiards arcade and mock gambling. The sale was expected to close in June 1996.

As of the writing of this book, nothing has changed in the external appearance of the historic Balinese Room.

Bamboo Room

2012 Market, Galveston, owner/operator, Pat Cotton. Was one of the 47 night spots listed in the June 11, 1957 injunctions. Gambling and liquor violations.

Band Box Club

804 North Boulevard Dr., Galveston, owner/operator, William D. Dennis. Was one of the 47 night spots listed in the June 11, 1957 injunctions. Gambling (slot machines) and liquor violations.

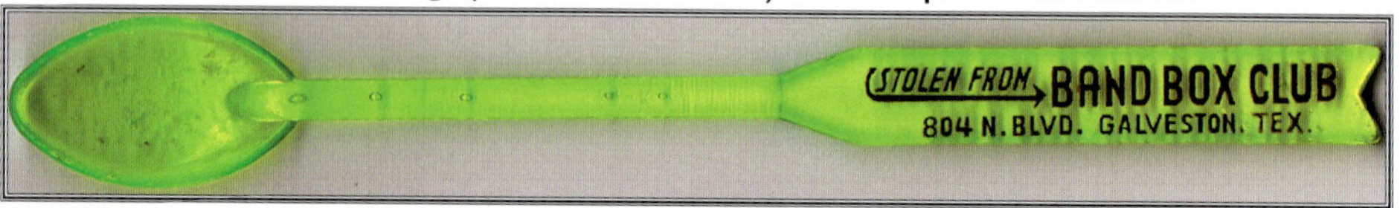

FEC # 65 Fluorescent plastic drink stir stick.

The Barge

Located on East Beach, Galveston, owner/operator, John L. "Johnny Jack" Nounes, aka, "The Beau Brummel of Galveston."

FEC # 66 Ad from November 3, 1950. Galveston Week.

Bay Club

The exact address and owner is unknown. It was a large club that fronted Galveston Bay in Kemah, according to Jim Simpson.

FEC # 67 OBV. & REV. Gray.

FEC # 68 OBV. & REV. Dark pink.

FEC # 69 OBV. & REV. Black.This chip was on a key chain. It's the only one known.

Beach Amusement Parlor

2202 Ave. Q, Galveston, owner/operator, Willie H. Wisco. Jim Simpson filed five more injunction suits 6/13/57 for permitting gambling and bingo. An add in July 18, 1952 Galveston Week stated it was, "The home of the big games. When you visit Willie's popular spot, you're a cinch to get plenty of entertainment."

FEC # 70 Ad in July 18, 1952.
Galveston Week.

Beach Club

2310 ½ Boulevard, Galveston, owner/operator, Van O. Martin and Jolla Walker. Was one of the 47 night spots listed in the June 11, 1957 injunctions. Gambling and liquor violations.

FEC # 71-A OBV. Black.

FEC # 71-B REV.

Beach Club

The (Galveston Texas Beach Club,) second floor of Crystal Palace. Entrances 2316 Seawall Boulevard and 2115 Tremont. Owner/operator, Vic A. (Gigolo) Maceo. It was also the home of the Crystal Palace Cafe. It was listed in 1941 city directory as 2300 Boulevard, Crystal Palace Bldg., ball room, bath house, apts. The crosswalk over Seawall Boulevard can be seen in many pictures.

FEC # 72 Crystal Palace and beach scene from old 1¢ post card.

FEC # 73 Ad from July 18, 1952. Galveston Week.

FEC # 74-A Matchbook, front cover.

FEC # 74-B Matchbook, back cover.

FEC # 74-C Matches inside.

FEC # 75-A OBV. Blue.

FEC # 75-B REV.

FEC # 76-A OBV. Tan.

FEC # 76-B REV.

FEC # 77-A OBV. Red.

FEC # 77-B REV.

FEC #78-A OBV. Gray.
Courtesy Vern Blanck.

FEC # 78-B REV.
Courtesy Vern Blanck.

Beacon Light

2012 Ave. E, Galveston, owner/operator, Hendrik Blok. The Houston Chronicle reported on 3/2/41, that Hendrik Blok pleaded guilty of permitting gambling and was fined $25 and plus court cost on 3/1/41, by Justice James A. Piperi. Charges filed by Texas Ranger J. A. Thompson.

Beckman's

One and a half miles south of Kemah, owner/operator, Horace Beckman. Was one of the 47 night spots listed in the June 11, 1957 injunctions. Gambling and liquor.

Big Brick

014 20th St., Galveston, owner/operator, Steve Oparenavich.

FEC # 79-A Matchbook, front cover.

FEC # 79-B Matchbook, back cover.

Bill's Grill

2102 26th St., Galveston, owner/operator, Bill Andrus.

FEC # 80 Ad from April 4, 1947.
Galveston Week.

Bird Cage

2227 Seawall Blvd., Galveston, owner/operator, TAC. It was atop Murdoch's Bath House and had eight or ten slot machines in a small room. May have been managed by Robert Lee Fabj.

Blue Room Club

1917 45th St., Galveston, owner/operator, Charley Battaglia.

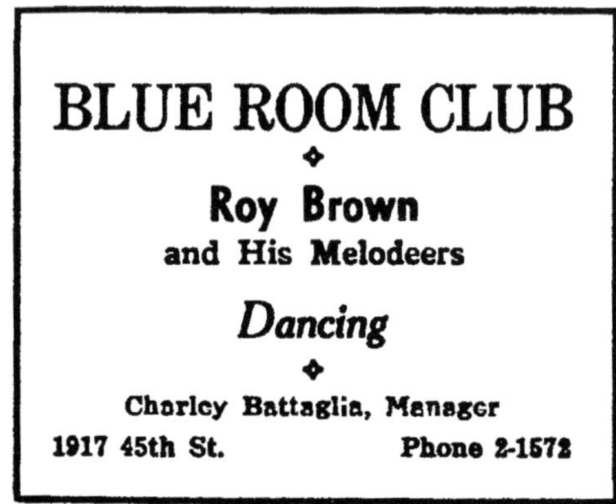

FEC # 81 Ad from April 4, 1947. Galveston Week.

Bonita Club

Kemah, owner/operator, W. E. "Red" Nelson. Jim Simpson filed five more injunction suits 6/13/57 for permitting gambling.

Boulevard Amusement

2308 and 2312 Seawall Blvd., Galveston, owner/operator, Fred W. McBride.

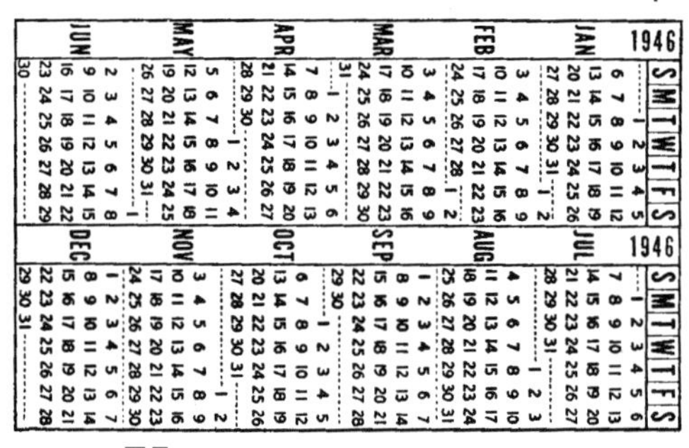

FEC # 82-A Calendar, dated 1946. It was in the deck of cards and has same back as the other cards in the deck.

FEC # 82-B Back of deck of cards.

FEC # 83 Glass ashtray.

Even though one has the address of 2312 and the other one is 2308, I believe they were the same business, at the same building.

Brass Rail

2312 Seawall Blvd., Galveston, owner/operator, Evalyn Wadsworth. Note the same address as the Boulevard Amusement in 1946.

Brownie's Casino

On Seawall Blvd., Galveston, owner/operator, unknown. It was an old club, close to Murdoch's Bath House and had gambling.

Cadillac Bar

2022 Ave. E, Galveston. owner/operator, James R. Peck and Earl LeCroy.

Cafe Sea Breeze

61st and Ave. O, Galveston, owners/operators, Diamond and Johnny's.

DIAMOND & JOHNNY'S

Cafe Sea Breeze

61st and O

Galveston's Most Popular Spot to Dine and Dance over the water.

SPECIALISTS IN FINE FOOD, STEAKS, CHICKEN, SEAFOODS AND FRENCH FRIED SHRIMP

FEC # 84 Ad from July 18, 1952. Galveston Week.

Capitol Bar

The Capitol Bar is reported to have been a black bar in Galveston, owner/operator, unknown. The chips are made of pressed paper.

FEC # 85-A OBV. Blue.

FEC # 85-B REV.

FEC # 86-A OBV. White.

FEC # 86-B REV.

Cedar Oaks Club

The club set about 400 yards off the road, down by a bayou in Dickinson. Owners/operators, Joe Jr., Mike, and Pete Salvato, Anthony J. and Victor J. Fertitta. Was one of the 47 night spots listed in the June 11, 1957 injunctions. Gambling and liquor violations. Joe Jr. was the older brother, Mike was a Marine in the Pacific, and was a very real war hero, Pete is the only surviving brother. The chip rack shown below is one of two the I have. It was purchased from Angelo J. Tramuto, a dealer that worked for the club. He also identified the SSS chips (Salvato brothers) as being used in the club.

FEC # 87 Dealer chip rack holds 1200 chips and has money box on each end. 27x7½x3½.

FEC # 88-A OBV. Yellow with blue water marks.

FEC # 88-B REV.

FEC # 89-A OBV. Black.

FEC # 89-B REV.

FEC # 90-A OBV. Red.

FEC # 90-B REV.

FEC # 91-A OBV. Tan.

FEC # 91-B REV.

Chesterfield Club

Address and owner/operator, unknown.

Chesterfield Club

invites you to attend its

Eighth Annual Dance

Friday evening, April thirtieth
Nineteen hundred and forty-eight
at Ten o'clock

Club Manhattan

Galveston, Texas

Formal

FEC # 92 Invitation to the Manhattan Club.
Dated 1948. See Manhattan Club # 174.

Chili Bowl

Next to the Kemah Den on the strip in Kemah, owner/operator, Vic A. Maceo (Gigolo) and Tom A. Fertitta (Tommie). Jim Simpson filed five more injunction suits 6/13/57 for permitting gambling. They had horse betting, bingo, and other forms of gambling.

Chop Suey

2107 Seawall Blvd. at 21st St., Galveston, owner/operator, Sam and Rose Maceo. They opened it in 1923, as their first attempt into the entertainment business. The building later became Maceo's Grotto in 1926, the Sui Jen in 1932, and the famed Balinese Room in 1942.

Circle Club

2327 Ave. F, Galveston, owner/operator, Elwood E. Talbott. Was one of the 47 night spots listed in the June 11, 1957 injunctions. Gambling and liquor violations.

FEC # 93 OBV. & REV. Tan.

Circle Z Bar

5801 Broadway at 58th, Galveston, owner/operator, Mr. and Mrs. R. C. Zorn.

Ciro's Club

2402 Seawall Blvd., Galveston, owner/operator, Jack O'Toole. Was one of the 47 night spots listed in the June 11, 1957 injunctions. Gambling and liquor violations.

Clock Club

2114½ Ave. D, Galveston, owner/operator, Vivian Licata. Was one of the 47 night spots listed in the June 11, 1957 injunctions. Gambling and liquor violations. In new raids on 6/18/57, Vincent Klevenhagen broke down the door and found several cases of tip books. At a news stand below the Clock Club, they found and shattered two pinball machines.

FEC # 94 OBV. & REV. Orange.

C.L.U.

Address and owner/operator unknown. Was one of the 47 night spots listed in the June 11, 1957 injunctions. Gambling and liquor violations.

Club

Address and owner/operator unknown. Was one of the 47 night spots listed in the June 11, 1957 injunctions. Gambling and liquor violations.

Club C

Was on the strip in Kemah, owner/operator, Johnny Johnson. Was one of the 47 night spots listed in the June 11, 1957 injunctions. Gambling and liquor violations. They had console slot machines at club.

FEC # 95 OBV. & REV. Light orange. Chip has a hole drilled in it.

Club Forest

414 24th, Galveston, owner/operator, Eddie Baker.

Club Show Time

61st and Ave. S, Galveston, owner/operator, Cliff Kellett.

FEC # 96 Ad from November 3, 1950. Galveston Week. Note the last show 2:30 A. M. They had to be open for gambling at that late hour.

Colony Club

There were two Colony Clubs. One was in Dickinson, owner/operator, Lee Woodson. The other Colony Club was at 20th and Strand, in Galveston, owner/operator, unknown. It is not known which chip was used in which club.

FEC # 97-A OBV. Burgundy.

FEC # 97-B REV.

FEC # 98-A OBV. Blue.

FEC # 98-B REV.

FEC # 99-A OBV. Brown.

FEC # 99-B REV.

Corral Club

2002 Ave. E, Galveston, owner/operator, Alf J.DelPapa.

Cosmo Club

2019 Market, Galveston, owner/operator, Munzo (Papa) Jamail.

FEC # 100 Ad from April 4, 1947. Galveston Week.

COSMO CLUB

MUSIC ★ ENTERTAINMENT

REFRESHMENTS

Phone 2-5316 2019 Market

MUNZO JAMAIL, Mgr.

Cottage Club

Kemah, address and owner/operator, unknown. Some old cronies in Dickinson told me about the club.

Cotton Club

Address and owner/operator, unknown, Galveston. Reported in Christie's Beachcomber, Galveston paper, 10/3/54.

Country Club

Robert Lee Fabj (Babby) had 1100 slot machines in a warehouse that belonged to the Country Club and the Artillery Club.

Cozy Rooms

Galveston, owner/operator, Jessie Elliott and Mary Russell. Was one of the 47 night spots listed in the June 11, 1957 injunctions. Bawdy house and liquor violations.

Cracker's Inn

1905 23rd St., Galveston, owner/operator, Marvin M. (Cracker) Brown. Cracker loaned the use of his convertible to the Jaycees to take the Miss Texas Beauty Pageant contestants to the ribbon cutting ceremony of, "Fifty miles of shining concrete," the Gulf Freeway, August 2, 1952.

Crystal Club

2406 Market St. Ave. D, Galveston, owner/operator, Patricia Byrd. (1955 City Directory.) Every yellow chip ever seen, has STOCKTON on it. Could have been used for a casino night, for mock gambling.

FEC # 101 Business card, circa unknown.

FEC # 102 OBV. & REV. Dark blue.

FEC # 103 OBV. & REV. Red.

FEC # 104 OBV. & REV. White.

FEC # 105 OBV. & REV. Yellow.

Darnell's

8022 1st St., Galveston, owner/operator, Marvin W. and Gloria Darnell. An ad in the 1955 City Directory advertised a room for private parties.

FEC # 106 Ad in November 3, 1950. Galveston Week.

De Elmos

Kemah, address and owner/operator, unknown. Bill Nelkin, owner, "Cola Collection" in the Village, told me about this club. All he could remember was the the club name and that it was in Kemah.

Del Mar

Address and owner/operator, unknown, Galveston. The Texas Rangers confiscated dice tables here in 1937.

De Luxe Club

2017 Ave. E, Galveston, owner/operator, Ollie J. and Snozzer Quinn.

FEC # 107 OBV. & REV. Blue.

FEC # 108 Matchbook front.
See Home Plate # 145 for inside.
See Pilot Bar # 190 for back.

FEC # 109-A OBV. Dark blue.

FEC # 109-B REV.

Dickinson Social Club

On Farm to Market Rd. 517, two miles southwest of Dickinson, owners/operators, Sam and Carlos Emmite, Joe Jr., Mike, and Pete Salvato, Anthony J. and Victor J. Fertitta. Was one of the 47 night spots listed in the June 11, 1957 injunctions. Gambling and liquor violations. Angelo J. Tramuto, a dealer that worked for the club, identified the EE chips (Emmite brothers) as being used in the club. The club was also known as D. & S.

FEC # 110-A OBV. Lavender.

FEC # 110-B REV.

FEC # 111-A OBV. Black.

FEC # 111-B REV.

FEC # 112-A OBV. Red.

FEC # 112-B REV.

FEC # 113-A OBV. Tan.
Same on $1 & 25¢.

FEC # 113-B REV.

FEC # 113-C REV.
Courtesy Vern Blanck.

FEC # 114-A OBV. Yellow.

FEC # 114-B REV.

Eagles Club

1906 Ave. E, Galveston, owner/operator, unknown.

Edgewater Lounge

Kemah, owner/operator, Anthony J. Fertitta and Tom A. Fertitta (Tommie). It was located inside Jimmie Walker Restaurant, that was at the junction of the Clear Lake yacht channel and Galveston Bay. It later became Willie G's, and is now Landry's, which is owned by Tilman Fertitta.

FEC # 115-A OBV. Lavender.

FEC # 115-B REV.

FEC # 116 OBV. & REV. Matchbook.

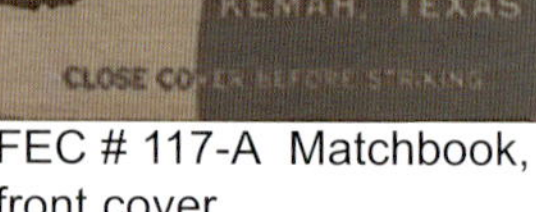

FEC # 117-A Matchbook, front cover.

FEC # 117-B Matchbook, back cover.

The initials ATF on the following chips are for Anthony and Tom Fertitta, who managed the Edgewater Lounge. The chips were used in the club, according to a gentleman, who was a dealer there.

FEC # 118-A OBV. Black.

FEC # 118-B REV.

FEC # 119-A OBV. Yellow.

FEC # 119-B REV.

Elks Club

1518 23rd, Galveston, owner/operator, unknown.

Embassy Club

2320 Postoffice, Galveston, owners/operators, Gus L. Sabanovich, Joe Forrest, and Sister Sophie. Was one of the 47 night spots listed in the June 11, 1957 injunctions. Gambling (black-jack) and liquor violations. Jim Simpson's men made mop-up raids here, when he filed five more injunctions suits for other clubs on 6/13/57.

FEC # 120 Ad from November 3, 1950. Galveston Week.

Esquire Club

2026 ½ Ave. E, Galveston, owner/operator, Doris Summerlin, aka, Doris Summerly. Was one of the 47 night spots listed in the June 11, 1957 injunctions. Gambling and liquor violations. Jim Simpson's men made mop-up raids here, when he filed five more injunctions suits for other clubs on 6/13/57.

FEC # 121 OBV. & REV. Lavender.

419 Club

419 24th St., Galveston, owner/operator, Dorothy (Dottie) Tyler. Was one of the 47 night spots listed in the June 11, 1957 injunctions. Gambling (slot machines) and liquor violations.

Fourth Estate Club

1913 23rd St., Galveston, owner/operator, Lee Woodson.

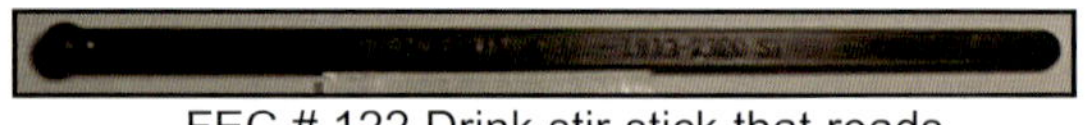

FEC # 122 Drink stir stick that reads.
FOURTH ESTATE CLUB - 1913 - 23RD ST

Fremont Club

This chip came out of Galveston, and I was told that it was on Market St., but he was unsure of the exact address.

FEC # 123-A OBV. Yellow.

FEC # 123-B REV.

Gaido's

Seawall Blvd., Galveston. The original owner/operator, was San Jacinto Gaido. He founded the restaurant in 1911 on Murdoch's Pier. It was, and is, probably one of the the finest seafood restaurant on the island. His descendants are the operators of the Gaido's Motel and Restaurant, just across the street from the from the old location. Gaido's was not a gambling club, but it did have a few slot machines at the request of Sam and Rose. They have a small collection of chips on display and a 1924, wide-angle photograph of Murdoch's bathhouse, in which the Chop Suey can be seen.

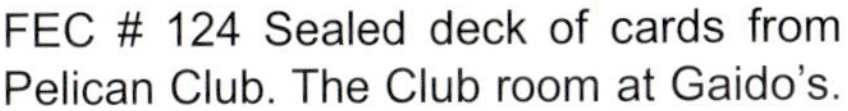
FEC # 124 Sealed deck of cards from Pelican Club. The Club room at Gaido's.

FEC # 125 Drink coaster, circa 1997.

Galveston Downs

Horse race betting became illegal in 1909, but Galveston Downs, near Offat's Bayou, was still up and running in the 1920's. It was converted to a dog track, but it finally closed before betting became legal again.

FEC # 126 Galveston Downs, circa 1920's.

Galveston Novelty Co

2005 23rd St., Galveston, owner/operator, TAC, John B. Arena and Robert Lee Fabj. On June 19, 1957 Texas Rangers found slot machines and tip books.

Galvez Hotel

1902 Seawall Blvd., Galveston, owners/operators. The

Galvez opened on June 10, 1911. It was built by the Galveston Street Railway Company and I. H. Kempner. Archie Bennett and Dr. Denton Cooley, of Houston, bought the Galvez in 1978 and restored it. It later became part of the Moody hotel chain.

Sam Maceo was living in his penthouse apartment at the Galvez, when W. L. Moody Jr. bought the hotel. Phil Harris and Alice Fay were married in Sam's penthouse in 1941. At the outbreak of WW II, the Coast Guard took over the Galvez. Sam and his new wife Edna moved to the Buccaneer Hotel. Sam ran card games for the big time spenders but as far as I can determine, there was no open gambling at the Galvez.

(1)

NOTICE OF PAYMENT DUE

The National Cash Register Company

Mail remittance to:

W. A. RYAN, Sales Agent

515 Caroline St.

Houston, Texas

A payment will be due on your note according to the terms of your contract as shown below. **PLEASE MAKE YOUR REMITTANCE PAYABLE TO THE ORDER OF THE NATIONAL CASH REGISTER COMPANY,** and mail it promptly with this notice to reach the agency office shown above on date due.

If the entire balance owing on this account is paid at one time, we will allow you 5% discount on that part not yet due, provided it consists of four or more payments. **(THIS IS NOT A RECEIPT)** **The National Cash Register Company**

Payer		Date of Promissory Note and N. C. R. Collection Symbol
S MACEO HOTEL GALVEZ GALVESTON TEX	7-18 S HOU	

Printed By a National Office Register	Date Due	Number	Amount Due
	JUN-18-29	(11)	25.00

FEC # 127 Bill to Sam Maceo from National Cash Register at Galvez Hotel, dated June 18, 1929.

FEC # 128 Key from the Galvez Hotel. Found for me by Lenette Heideman.

FEC # 129-A Matchbook, front.

FEC # 129-B Matchbook, back.

FEC # 130-A One piece 6" x 3" cup and dish from the Galvez Hotel. Its use is unknown. It could have been for shucked oysters or crab meat.

FEC # 130-B Manufacturer's stamp on bottom of cup-dish. Note spelling. Galver instead of Galvez.

Gateway Club

6002 Ave. R, half block off 61st, St., Galveston, owner/operator, Otis D. Skains. Note, they were open until 6:00 A. M.

Dine and Dance

☆

GATEWAY CLUB

6002 AVENUE R

Half Block Off 61st Street

☆

HANK PREE

and HIS ORCHESTRA

Play 9 p.m. to 4 a.m.

☆

Nightly Radio Broadcast Over
KLUF From 11:00 to 11:30

☆

SIRLOIN STRIPS

☆

OPEN TILL 6 A. M.

Phone 2-0753 Reservation — J. H. "Friday" Perdue, Manager

FEC # 131 Ad from April 4, 1947. Galveston Week.

Gay Kat

2828 Ave. R ½, Galveston, owner/operator, Arnette and Mrs. Eva Goolsby.

FEC # 132 OBV. & REV. Yellow.

Golden Greek Private Club

Address unknown, owner/operator, Paul Santire. Paul was also listed with the Crystal Palace Cafe in the 1955 City Directory.

THIS HEREBY CERTIFIES THAT H-No Expiration

Capt. A.W. Durrett No. 323

IS A MEMBER OF AND IS ENTITLED TO ALL CLUB PRIVILEGES OF THE

GOLDEN GREEK PRIVATE CLUB
GALVESTON, TEXAS

Paul Santire
Managing Director

This is a permanently valid Membership Card unless lost, stolen or revoked for violation of Club By-Laws.

FEC # 133 Membership card, circa 1950's. The 1955 City Directory listed an Alf W. Durrett as a boat captain.

Golden Pheasant

Hwy. 3 and 517, Dickinson, owner/operator, the Termini family. It sat on the corner of Hwy. 3 and Main St., across the street from what is now, Queen of Angles Catholic Church. There is now a Shell station on the lot. On some days, you could barely get by this intersection for the cars and traffic.

FEC # 134 OBV. & REV. Yellow.

Greek American Club

Galveston, owner/operator, unknown. Dutch Voight and his cohort, Ollie J. Quinn, gambled here in early days.

The Green Door

Address, owner/operator, unknown. Reported to be in San Leon, by Linda Mendez.

The Grotto

2107 Seawall Boulevard at 21st Street, Galveston, owner/operator, Sam and Rose Maceo and Dutch Voight. It was first the Chop Suey in 1923, then opened as the Grotto in 1926. Closed 1928 for gaming violation, damaged by storm in 1932, remodeled, it was opened as the Sui Jen in the same year. Then it became the famed Balinese Room in 1942. The Grotto had a dance pavilion called the Garden of Tokio.

Gulf Room

2227 Seawall Blvd., Galveston, owner/operator, TAC. It was atop Murdoch's famous pier and had gambling.

Gulf Towers Lounge

1921 Moody Ave., Galveston, owner/operator, Claude K. and Mary F. Swaringer. It was in the Golf Towers Hotel. Was one of the 47 night spots listed in the June 11, 1957 injunctions. Liquor violations.

FEC # 135 Ad from July 18, 1952. Galveston Week.

Handy's Place

2815 Ave. D, Galveston, owner/operator Joe Handy.

Happy's News Stand

2114 Market, Galveston, owner/operator, Vincent Genna. Chief Hanson broke up two pinball machines on 6/18/57 in new raids. In another raid on 6/19/57 they found slot machines and tip books.

Harmony Hangout

621 21st St., Galveston, owner/operator, Ruth T. Wasson.

Hollywood Dinner Club

6102 Ave. S, Galveston, at 61st, just outside the city limits, owner/operator, Sam and Rose Maceo, Dutch Voight, and Ollie J. Quinn. The club opened in 1926, closed and padlocked by a court injunction in 1939, after lawmen found narcotics on some of the patrons. It burned down on 8/13/59. There was dinner seating for 500, a large dance floor, thirty crap tables, and a wide array of other gambling devices. A gas station sets on the lot today.

FEC # 136 The HDC in its heyday. Courtesy of Rosenberg Library, Galveston, Texas.

Guy Lombardo pulled 20,000 customers during a three week stand at the club. Other stars that preformed there were Frank Sinatra, Bob Hope, Jack Benny, George Burns and Gracie Allen, Glen Miller, Rat Noble, Jack Dempsey, Phil Harris, Spike Jones, Shep Fields, and Duke Ellington to name a few. Fred Astaire and Arthur Murray also judged dance contests and gave free dance lessons, as they did at the Balinese Room.

FEC # 137 Tablecloth from HDC. Courtesy Angelo Montalbano.

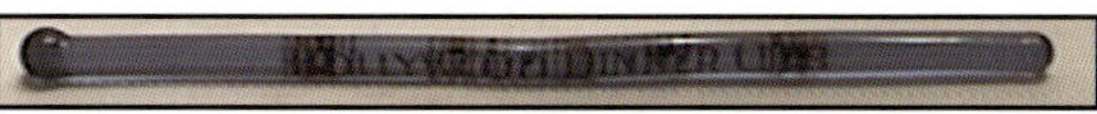

FEC # 138 Blue cobalt drink stir stick that reads.
HOLLYWOOD DINNER CLUB
SAM MACEO Managing Dir.
GALVESTON, TEXAS

Ben Bernie, during a nationwide radio hook-up, adlibbed that, “Am I welcome here? Even the water is coming to greet me.” The Hollywood was surrounded by two feet of seawater from a hurricane that was raging outside.

A desperate band leader came up short a member of his orchestra one evening and hired a Beaumont trumpeter, his name was Harry James. Frank Battaglia was the headwaiter at the HDC.

FEC # 139 The HDC on the northwest corner of Stewart Rd. and 61st Street. Closed and neglected, in this 1957 photo. Courtesy of Rosenberg Library, Galveston, Texas.

Linda Mendez, a fellow member of the Greater Houston Casino Chip and Gaming Token Collectors Club, related this account to me at one of our meetings recently. She was in junior high school in Galveston during the 50's. Linda had a friend, Ellabeth Hencey, that lived close to the intersection of Stewart Rd. and 61st St. The girls knew about the big building that used to be a nightclub and gambling casino, but it had been closed since 1939. They remembered hearing their parents talk about the Hollywood Dinner Club and all the big named stars that had preformed there over the years. Linda added, that she had gone to school with some of the Maceo decedents. The girls had always wanted to go into the place. One day, they discovered they could get under the large iron gate that was across the main entrance driveway. They crawled under the gate and went up to the building. The girls found a door where they could go in. Once in, the defunct Hollywood Dinner Club became their place to play.

Linda said the place was full of stuff. Autographed photos of the stars that had preformed in the club were hanging on the walls. There were slot machines and other gambling paraphernalia. Hollywood Dinner Club bills and gambling chips were strewn on the floor. Linda said it looked like everybody had just walked out and a big wind swept through the place and blew everything around. She now wishes she had picked up some of the items. Linda's father was very straight laced. He was anti-gambling and Maceo. Linda didn't want her parents to find out that they were sneaking in there to play, so she couldn't take anything home, less they would have been found out.

Linda's father's first cousin, whom he was raised with, was in the Galveston Fire Department. Consequently, her father would get a phone call whenever there was a large fire on the island. On August 13, 1959, they got a call and off they went. Her dad took her to the Hollywood Dinner Club. It was ablaze. Linda stood beside her father watching the firemen fight the flames and began crying. Her dad asked her, "What is wrong with you," but all she could say was, "Well, it was just a neat building."

Linda was talking to her father recently and told him about how they used to go in the Hollywood Dinner Club to play and that she is now collects gambling chips. He asked her if she remembered when the police and the Texas Rangers came to the house next door. Her dad said the guy had several slot machines he was storing in his garage from the Hollywood Dinner Club. She said she remembered them going in there and tearing up the garage, but she didn't know just what they were doing.

Ellabeth Hencey is the current owner of the famous Star Drug Store at 510 & 512, 23rd Street, in Galveston. She also owns the Moulin Rouge Club and other historic building on the island.

FEC # 140 OBV. & REV. Red.

FEC # 141 OBV. & REV. Black.
Courtesy Angelo Montalbano.

I acquired this chip from a man in Galveston, along with many other known Galveston chips (TAC). He told me that these and the other chips, came out of a Maceo warehouse. It is the same design and age as the Fremont Club chip.

FEC # 142 OBV. & REV. Tan.

FLOOR SHOW nightly
with THE VERNONS
Evelyne and James
SUNDAYS:
DINNER MUSIC WITH NO COUVERT CHARGE
TO DINNER GUESTS FROM 6 TO 9 PM
FLOOR SHOW AT 8:30
COUVERT CHARGES TO ALL GUESTS
REMAINING AFTER 9 O'CLOCK
MAKE YOUR RESERVATIONS NOW!
for GALA NEW YEAR'S EVE PARTY
at
HOLLYWOOD DINNER CLUB
Dec. 31st

FEC # 143 Double sided placard, see Sui Jen # 258 for other side.

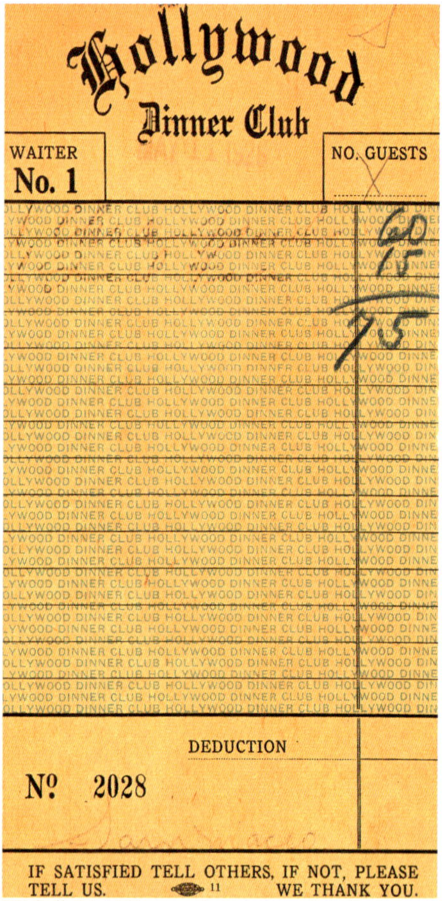

Hollywood
Dinner Club
WAITER No. 1
NO. GUESTS
DEDUCTION
No. 2028
IF SATISFIED TELL OTHERS, IF NOT, PLEASE TELL US. WE THANK YOU.

FEC # 144 Dinner check from HDC, dated May 11, 1929. Signed by Sam Maceo.

Home Plate Cigar Stand

2024 Ave. E, Galveston, owner/operator, Ollie J. Quinn. Had horse betting and other gambling.

FEC # 145 Matchbook inside.
See De Luxe Club # 108 for front.
See Pilot Bar # 190 for back.

Hope Rooms

Address unknown, Galveston, owner/operator, Jessie Elliott. Jim Simpson filed five more injunction suits 6/13/57 for bawdy house and open saloon.

Horseshoe Club

1012 37th St., Galveston, owner/operator, Cotton Guerrant. Jim Simpson filed five more injunction suits 6/13/57 for gambling and open bar.

FEC # 146 OBV. & REV. Yellow.

Howl Club

1403 Ave. B, Galveston, owner/operator, Betty Richardson and Mary W. McGibony. Was one of the 47 night spots listed in the June 11, 1957 injunctions. Gambling and liquor.

Hurricane Club

214 21st St., Galveston, owner/operator, John F. Moriarty and Yvonne Simonsen. Was one of the 47 night spots listed in the June 11, 1957 injunctions. Gambling (dice) and liquor.

Idle Hour Club

1903 23rd St., Galveston, owner/operator, John F. Moriarty and Harold Haven. Was one of the 47 night spots listed in the June 11, 1957 injunctions. Gambling (slot machines and blackjack) and liquor.

FEC # 147 Plastic drink stir stick that reads.
IDLE HOUR LOUNGE
1903-23RD. SO 3-9431

Imperial Club

2319 Post Office, Ave. E, Galveston, owner/operator, Joe T. Hanson. Also known as The Imperial Club and Tavern, 2317 Post Office, Ave. E, and The Imperial Athletic Association Club. Was one of the 47 night spots listed in the June 11, 1957 injunctions. Gambling (slot machines and blackjack) and liquor. It was also hit in the mop-up raids on 6/13/57. Glen Campbell performed at the Imperial when he was 14 years old, about 1952, when the city was wide open. Club was about two blocks outside red light district. The club had a ill-omened nickname, “The Bucket of Blood.” Johnny Cash and Roy Acuff played at the club from time to time.

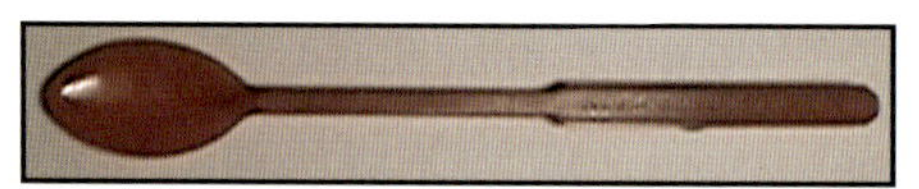

FEC # 148 Plastic drink stir stick that reads.
JOE’S IMPERIAL CLUB
GALVESTON, TEXAS

FEC # 149 OBV. & REV. Red.

FEC # 150 Ad from November 3, 1950. Galveston Week.

FEC # 151 OBV. & REV. Blue.

FEC # 152 OBV. & REV. Orange.

Interurban Queen Cigar and News Stand

624 21st St. until 1934, 2027 Market for 13 years, then moved a few doors away in 1947 to 2019 Market, Galveston, closed in 1992, owner/operator, Chris Tellefson and Tom McKenna.

INTERURBAN QUEEN
CIGAR AND NEWS
STAND

Visit Our Curio Shop

2027 Market Phone 2-2421

FEC # 153 Ad from April 4, 1947. Galveston Week.

FEC # 154 Ad from July 18, 1952. Galveston Week.

The second location was on the southwest corner of 21st St. and Market. Douglas "Wrong Way" Corrigan was born in the building above the store's site. When Corrigan returned to his birth place, shortly after his historic flight to Ireland, he visited the shop and was shown the approximately seven thousand curios Tellefson had on display. When I visited the store in the early 1990's, very few items were left. Dick Waterman, who was running the store, was also managing the Old Galveston Club, that was in the back of the building. Both businesses were on the same floor. You could go from one business to the other, by just going through a door. Dick told me the history and showed me some of the items that were remaining. There were small tables with numbers on them. Dick said that slot machines once sat on the tables. In the Old Galveston Club there were tables, with design of a painter's palette, that came out of the Studio Lounge. We traded some items. I got some chips and a tip board, along with some other good stuff.

FEC # 155 Photo of curio shop at Interurban Queen. Galveston Isle Magazine November, 1947.

OPEN (409) 765-6936
10 A.M. TO 2 A.M.

Old Galveston Club, Inc.

"The Last of the old Speakeasys"

BELLY UP TO
THE 1884 BAR
SEE THE BOSS

2019 MARKET (REAR)
GALVESTON, TX 77550

FEC # 156 Business card.

Carriage Gate Promotions

Dick Waterman

P.O. Drawer T.
Galveston, Texas 77552

(409) 765-6936
(409) 765-6625

FEC # 157 Business card.

The Old Galveston Club closed in 1992. The remaining contents of the Old Galveston Club and the Interurban Queen were sold at an auction. I could not attend the auction, but placed some sealed bids. I'm sorry to say, I was out bid on every item. The building was razed by the American National Insurance Company to built an employee parking lot on the land. Another Island treasure that is lost for all time.

FEC # 158 Tip board from the Interurban Queen and the Old Galveston Club.

FEC # 159 Paper trade tokens. REV. on left side, OBV. on right side.

Jack Tar Hotel

6th St. and Seawall Blvd., Galveston, owner/operator, Ed C. Leach. It is unknown if there was any gambling, but Jack Tar was a big name on the island.

FEC # 160 Post card, circa 1950's.

FEC # 161 Glass ashtray.

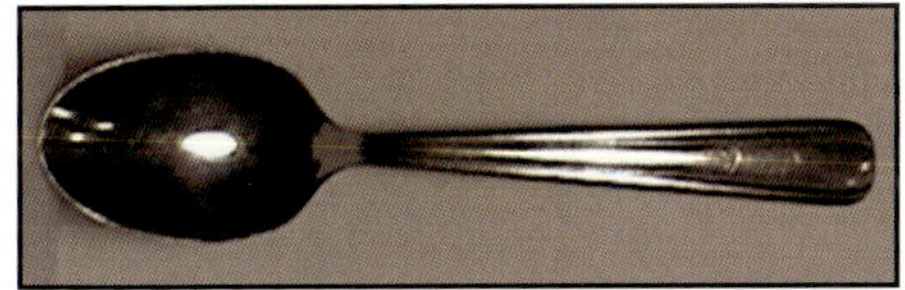

FEC # 162 Spoon from silverware set.

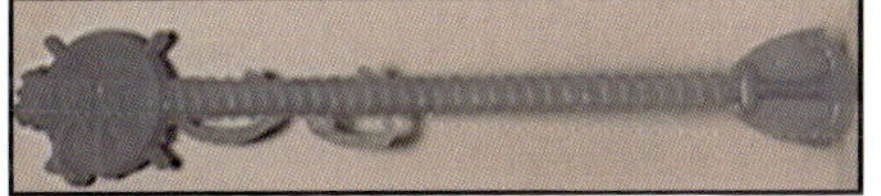

FEC # 163 Plastic drink stir stick.

Jean Davis's House

One mile north of the Texas City corporate limits, owner/operator, Jean and Buster Davis, of Clear Lake Shores Addition, Kemah. Was one of the 47 night spots listed in the June 11, 1957 injunctions. Bawdy house and liquor violations.

Jockey Club

705 37th St., Galveston, owner/operator, George Criss. On March 2, 1941, the Houston Chronicle reported that on March 1, 1941, in Galveston, George Criss pleaded guilty of permitting gambling, and was fined $25 plus court cost, by Justice James A. Piperi. The charges were filed by Texas Ranger, J. A. Thompson.

Kemah Club

Kemah, owner/operator, unknown. Some locals in Dickinson told me about the place.

Kemah Coffee Club

Address unknown, Kemah, owner/operator, Joe "Blow". Pinky Hull told me that it was a more recent place.

Kemah Den

Next to Chili Bowl on the strip in Kemah, owner/operator, Rose Dispensa. I have been told they did not have gambling in the club, but that they would take you by car, to private houses to gamble. Could this have been the club in Kemah that Givens and Yaws went to?

FEC # 164 Ad from July 18, 1952. Galveston Week.

FEC # 165 OBV. & REV. Green.

FEC # 166 OBV. & REV. Red.

Kit-Kat Garden

61st and Stewart Rd., Galveston, owner/operator, unknown. A dancer, named Ginger Rodgers, quit the Kit-Kat Club and ran off to California, with a clothes salesman from E. S. Levy & Co.

FEC # 167-A OBV.

FEC # 167-B REV.

L & M Club

1314 29th St., Galveston, owner/operator, Wilbur Henderson. It was raided on 6/14/57 by the Texas Rangers. They found race-horse machines, poker tables, dice tables and slot machines.

La Rumba Club

2712 Ave. D, Galveston, owner/operator, Frank Remero.

Lido Club

2016½ 23rd St., Galveston, owner/operator, unknown.

FEC # 168 Ad from August 9-16, 1946. This Week in Galveston.

Lido Club

COZY AND INTIMATE SPOT TO SPEND
A FEW PLEASANT HOURS

Second Floor, 2016½ 23rd

Upstairs

Phone 2-9016

Little Club

Address unknown, Galveston, owner/operator, unknown. Dutch Voight and Ollie J. Quinn gambled here in the early days. The Texas Rangers confiscated dice tables in 1937.

Little Turf

23rd St., left off of Seawall Blvd., Galveston, owner/operator, Abe T. Rosenthal, 1945 to 1947. Robert Lee Fabj took over after that. It is where the Club 23 is today, in the back of a L-shaped, two story building. The Little Turf was open Christmas 1938. Leo Lera, who shot Harry T. Phillips Christmas Eve, at a bar on Seawall Blvd., worked there.

FEC # 169 OBV. & REV. Tan.
Courtesy Angelo Montalbano.

FEC # 170 OBV. & REV. Black.
Courtesy Angelo Montalbano.

Lloyd's Club

2205 Ave. C, Galveston, owner/operator, Conley Lloyd, Manager, Robert Schmidt. George Buschong and Pinky Hull played the piano at the club. It was a large club, with exquisite food.

Lloyd's ***of Galveston CLUB***

proudly presents

BOBBY TINTEROW

AND HIS RHYTHMIC QUARTET

★ DINNER MUSIC NIGHTLY ★

2205 Avenue C **Phone 2-4433**

FEC # 171 Ad from April 4, 1947. Galveston Week.

FEC # 172-A OBV. White.

FEC # 172-B REV.

FEC # 173-A OBV. Black.
Courtesy Vern Blanck.

FEC # 173-B REV.
Courtesy Vern Blanck.

Lucky Club

408 21st St., Galveston, owners/operators, Pete Bernard and Fred Luckie, Was one of the 47 night spots listed in the June 11, 1957 injunctions. Liquor violations.

M & M Music Co.

Galveston, owner/operator, TAC, Vincent Jenna. Texas Ranger Johnny Klevenhagen smashed twenty-one slot machines and four pinball machines here.

Manhattan Club

2804½ Ave. R½, Galveston, owner/operator, Rudolph E. Wiley.

FEC # 174 Invitation to the Manhattan Club. Dated 1948. See Chesterfield Club # 92.

Chesterfield Club

invites you to attend its

Eighth Annual Dance

Friday evening, April thirtieth
Nineteen hundred and forty-eight
at Ten o'clock

Club Manhattan
Galveston, Texas

Formal

Marine Exchange Social Club

303 21st St., Galveston, owner/operator, Thomas W. Leach.

Marine Room

2227 Seawall Blvd., Galveston, owner/operator, TAC. It was atop Murdoch's famous pier. "Galveston has a national reputation because of its night life and the three big stars in the island's bright night clubs skies are the Studio Lounge, the Balinese Room, and the Marine Room. It has the largest air-condition ballroom in the Southwest." Galveston Isle Magazine, June 1950. Pier manager Jack Mankey and Irving Ducoff, with Henry Foster as seal keeper.

Toast of the Town...

TOMMY REED

and his orchestra

Featuring SUE MARO

AIR CONDITIONED
MARINE ROOM
GALVESTON'S
PLEASURE PIER

DANCING NIGHTLY 9 P.M. TO 1 A.M.

$1 Per Person Nightly, Except Saturdays and Holiday Eves ($2 Per Person) and Mondays ($1 Per Couple) Tax Included.

FEC # 175 Ad from July 18, 1952. Galveston Week.

Melody Club

2010 27th St., Galveston, owners/operators, Dan and Peggy Torres. Was one of the 47 night spots listed in the June 11, 1957 injunctions. Liquor violations.

FEC # 176 Ad from July 18, 1952. Galveston Week.

Metropole Club

4125 Ave. S, Galveston, owners/operators, Charley Burdee and Dorothy B. Graham. Was one of the 47 night spots listed in the June 11, 1957 injunctions. Liquor violations. It was at the end of Ave. S and would later become the late Bubby Kirk's Steak House.

FEC # 177 Ad from July 18, 1952. Galveston Week.

Mexican Joe's

Galveston, "It was on the second floor of a building on 23rd St. and was a favorite of the University of Texas Medical Branch students for its large dice table, where they could play for quarters." From an article, Class of '30, by Cyril V. Black, M.D. Dutch Voight and Ollie J. Quinn gambled here in early days.

Mint Club

1821 45th St., Galveston, owner/operator, Kevin M. Foley. Was one of the 47 night spots listed in the June 11, 1957 injunctions.

Mother Harvey's

2528 Postoffice, Galveston, owner/operator, Mother Harvey. The 1955 City Directory listed Charles T. Long as the householder. He also ran the Tipo Club at 2604 Ave. D. The house was also known as the Mollie Walters House. Mollie moved here from New Orleans after the Civil War, built the house in about 1886 and ran the brothel. She died in 1908 and the house was run by other madams until 1957. The house is now on the city's historic homes tour.

FEC # 178 Mother Harvey's on day of tours. Circa 1997.

Moulin Rouge Club

2212½ Mechanic St., Galveston, owner/operator, Vic A. Maceo. Was one of the 47 night spots listed in the June 11, 1957 injunctions. Gambling and liquor. It was also raided in the mop-up raids on 6/13/57. Ellabeth Hencey is the current owner of the Moulin Rouge Club.

FEC # 179 Ad from November 3, 1950. Galveston Week.

Murdoch's Bath House

2227 Seawall Blvd., Galveston, owner/operator, TAC. There were many operations at Murdoch's. They had bingo, horse betting, slot machines, and amusements. There was the Gulf Room, Murdoch's Cafe, Paul's News Stand, Electric Studio Photograph, Guyette's Gift Shop, Murdoch's Sportland, Galveston Beach Association, Galveston Beach Public Address System, Warren Richard Shoe Shine, The Deck Restaurant, and at one time Gaido's Restaurant, and Rose Maceo's Barber Shop.

FEC # 180 Photo from an old one ¢ post card.

FEC # 181 Matchbook back. See Turf Tap Room # 297 for front.

FEC # 182 Matchbook back. See Turf Grill # 283 for front.

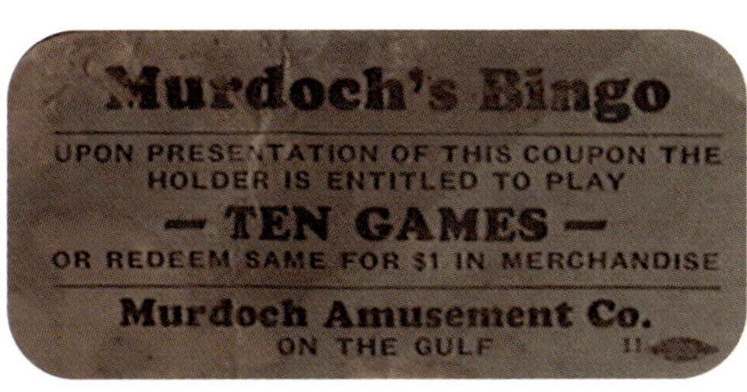

FEC # 183 Paper bingo check.

FEC # 184 Metal bingo token. Note spelling of Murdoch's.

Old Galveston Club

21st St. and Postoffice, Galveston, see Interurban Queen Cigar and News Stand.

Omar Khayyam Club

2016½ 23rd St., Galveston, owner/operator, Ernie and Rudolph Cevero. Was one of the 47 night spots listed in the June 11, 1957 injunctions. Gambling and liquor.

FEC # 185 Ad from July 18, 1952. Galveston Week.

One Star Tavern

2727 Ave. G, Galveston, owner/operator, Charlie Marshall.

FEC # 186 OBV. & REV. Red.

Palace Club

2014 Ave. E, Galveston, owner/operator, James W. (Woody) Walker. Was one of the 47 night spots listed in the June 11, 1957 injunctions. Gambling and liquor. The Houston Chronicle March 2, 1941, reported that in Galveston on March 1, 1941, Woody Walker pleaded guilty of permitting gambling, and was fined $25 plus court cost, by Justice James A. Piperi. Charges filed by Texas Ranger J. A. Thompson.

PALACE CLUB

The spot with continuous music and entertainment

•

WE NEVER CLOSE

•

Woody Walker, Mgr.

2014 Postoffice Phone 2-4511

FEC # 187 Ad from April 4, 1947. Galveston Week.

Peaches' Place

2827 Ave. H, Galveston, owner/operator, A. W. Heard. It was raided 6/14/57 by the Texas Rangers, who broke up a poker game and found racehorse machines and dice tables.

Peacock Cafe

416 21st St., Galveston, owner/operator, James C. and Nicholas K. Pratley.

FEC # 188 Glass ashtray.

Perusina Cafe and Tap Room

2214 Ave. C, Galveston, owner/operator, Jimmie E. Perusina, Joseph Bonario, and Fidel Ramentol.

2214 AVENUE C

FAMOUS THROUGHOUT THE SOUTHWEST FOR SIZZLING STEAKS, OYSTERS, SEA FOOD AND CHICKEN DISHES

OPEN FROM 7 A.M. TO 9 P.M.

FEC # 189 Ad from November 3, 1950. Galveston Week.

Phil Flake's Bingo Parlor

Galveston, State Representative Jean Horsey tried to block a restraining against the bingo parlor on 6/14/57.

Pilot Bar

425 21st St., Galveston, owner/operator, Mrs. Sarah Quinn.

FEC # 190 Matchbook back.
See De Luxe Club # 108 for front.
See Home Plate # 145 for inside,

PILOT BAR

★

STOP IN WITH
YOUR FRIENDS
for a COLD ONE

★

425 21st St. Phone 2-4141

FEC # 191 Ad from July 18, 1952.
Galveston Week.

Ping Pong Club

35th and Blvd., Galveston, owner/operator, Albert Doveri.

FEC # 192-A OBV.
Courtesy Bill Ray.

FEC # 192-B REV.
Courtesy Bill Ray.

FEC # 193 Ad from November 3, 1950.
Galveston Week.

Pirate Club

2214 Ave. Q, Galveston, owner/operator, Louise V. Burr. It was behind the Buccaneer Hotel and had a large purple neon sign. Was one of the 47 night spots listed in the June 11, 1957 injunctions. Gambling (slot machines) and liquor. It was also hit in the 6/13/57 mop-up raids.

FEC # 194 Ad from July 18, 1952. Galveston Week.

Playland Amusements

6114 Broadway, Galveston, owner/operator, TAC, Philip S. Flake. Was one of the 47 night spots listed in the June 11, 1957 injunctions. Gambling and liquor.

FEC # 195 Plastic key chain.

FEC # 196 Plastic girls wallet.

Rainbow Club

114/116 20th St., Galveston, owner/operator, Joseph J. Slemensky. Was one of the 47 night spots listed in the June 11, 1957 injunctions. Gambling and liquor. The Houston Chronicle reported on 3/2/41, that in Galveston on 3/1/41, Manuel Caballero pleaded guilty of permitting gambling and was fined $25 plus court cost by Justice James A. Piperi. Charges filed by Texas Ranger J. A. Thompson.

Rialto Club

411 25th St., Galveston, owner/operator, Omer B. Coate.

Tops in Entertainment
at the
RIALTO CLUB
Featuring the
RUSSELL LEWIS
Combo
and the
singing of
Ed Mitchell
411 25th • Dial 3-9972

FEC # 197 Ad from July 18, 1952. Galveston Week.

Ranch House

Three quarters of a mile west of Kemah, owner/operator, Mrs. D. A. Jones. Was one of the 47 night spots listed in the June 11, 1957 injunctions. Gambling and liquor.

Reno Club

2106 Ave. D, Galveston, owners/operators, Patsy DeCarlo, aka, Pasquale DeCarlo, Charles Bernard, and Frank Pinachio. Was one of the 47 night spots listed in the June 11, 1957 injunctions. Gambling and liquor.

FEC # 198 Ad from November 3, 1950. Galveston Week.

FEC # 199 OBV. & REV. Orange.

Resort Pavilion

Galveston, owner/operator, unknown. It was an older club that was located close to Murdoch's and had gambling.

Ricksha Room

800 University Blvd., Galveston, owner/operator, Diamond S., Peter S., John S., and Riley Athanasiou. Was one of the 47 night

spots listed in the June 11, 1957 injunctions. Gambling (console slot machines) and liquor. Peter had gotten out of the business on 4/20/57, so Jim Simpson moved to drop the charges against him.

FEC # 200-A Front of undated menu. A filet mignon was $4.50.

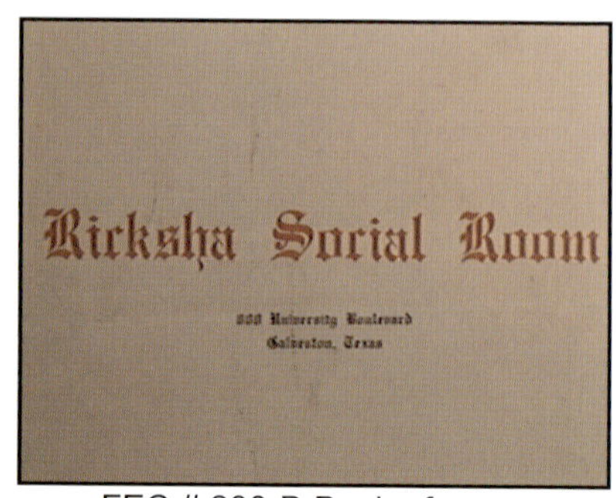

FEC # 200-B Back of menu.

FEC # 201 Photo of ricksha from Ricksha Room, taken at an auction held by the Galveston Historical Foundation where it was sold.

Rio Grande Club

2715 Market St., owner/operator, Jesse Lopez. In a raid on 6/17/57, they found thirty electronic slot machines, roulette wheels, dice, chips, and cards. On 6/18/57 they found more slot machines and tip books.

Dining and Dancing

FROM 5:00 P.M. 'TIL ?

Johnny Garcia

His Piano and His
Recording Latin-American
Band

PANCHITO RODRIGUEZ
Mexico's Singing Troubadour

THE FINEST MEXICAN FOODS
Served 24 Hours Daily in Our Cafe
THE HOME OF RUMBA MUSIC

RIO GRANDE CLUB & CAFE

Phone 3-9738 2715 Market Street

FEC # 202 Ad from July 18, 1952. Galveston Week.

Rod & Gun Club

61 St. and Ave. S, Galveston, across the street from the Hollywood Dinner Club, owner/operator, Lee Woodson.

The Rod and Gun Club

DINING ROOM

BETTER FOODS — A LITTLE DIFFERENT

Open 11 A. M.—Close 3.30 A. M

61st and Avenue S — Phone 6006

FEC # 203 Ad from August 9-16, 1946. This Week in Galveston.

Otis D. Skains reopened the club around 1947, at 2101 23rd St.

GALVESTON WEEK
Recommends
Otis Skains'
SUPER STEAKS AND FOOD AT THE
ROD & GUN CLUB
AIR CONDITIONED
Back of Buccaneer Hotel

FEC # 204 Ad from July 18, 1952. Galveston Week.

Was one of the 47 night spots listed in the June 11, 1957 injunctions. Gambling and liquor. William T. Gooding and Mrs. Louise Gooding were named in the June 11, 1957 injunctions.

Rodeo Club

It was on Hwy. 3, Dickinson, across from Roger's Malt Shop near Texas City, owner/operator, Mona Blanton. Therese Deats, reported August 14, 1995 for the Galveston Daily News. "Many of the oil field crews and workers made this their place to stop."

THE RODEO CLUB
THE HOME OF "NEVER A DULL MOMENT"

On the Kemah Highway
Near Texas City

MONA BLANTON, Manager

FEC # 205 Ad from November 3, 1950. Galveston Week.

Rose Garden

Close to the corner of Hwy. 3 and Deats Rd., Dickinson, just south of the Silver Moon, stood a two-story brick building, the Rose Garden. You could eat inside or they had car hops who would come to and wait on you. The second story was for gambling. They would have long limousines pull up and a load of what appeared to be

Captains and Officers, off a ship, file into the front door. It was owned by the Sam Giamfortone.

In the "Good old Days"

Anthony Tramuto stands in front of the Old Rose Garden before the Dickinson landmark was demolished. Tramuto had worked for the Giamfortone brothers prior to buying the building, which he has recently had torn down.

Landmark demolished

By BEVERLY MILLER
News Staff Writer

If sticks and stones could talk, what stories they could tell. They are all that remains of the Old Rose Garden on Highway 3 and Deats Road as the 57 year old building fell to the wrecker's ball two weeks ago. With its disappearance have gone many unspoken memories of the Dickinson that used to be, when gambling was king in the county and Dickinson was a star in its crown.

Opened as a cafe in 1926 by the late Sam Giamfortone, who took his $500 World War I bonus and obtained additional financing to build it, the upstairs gambling casino was added to the Old Rose Garden when Joe and Frank Giamfortone joined their brother in the business in 1937.

The casino was closed for gambling in 1939-40, and was used only for bingo for a time.

Reopening as a casino in 1944, the Old Rose Garden was known as one of the "hottest" clubs in the area, until it was closed for good when state Attorney General Will Wilson shut down gambling in Galveston County.

In 1962 Angelo Tramuto bought the building from Sam Giamfortone and put his real estate office in the ground floor.

"It needed to be torn down," said Nancy Knape, Tramuto's daughter. "It was so dilapidated, and it was a fire hazard," she said firmly.

Knape has opened a hair styling shop on the property, "and my Dad says he will build something else in place of the Old Rose Garden at a later date," Knape said.

If sticks and stones could talk, those who are more recent arrivals in Dickinson would know what used to be. With the wrecker's ball has gone a piece of history and not a small part of the lives of many people. Remaining are memories of the Dickinson that was. Encroaching rapidly is the Dickinson that will be. One will not replace the other.

Sam Giamfortone

FEC # 206 Undated clipping from unknown newspaper. Courtesy Angelo Tramuto.

The Rose Garden was later owned by Sam and Joe Jiambo in 1944 and closed in 1957. Philip Barderia, Joe Jiambo's nephew, was the owner after Joe died. Angelo Tramuto bought it in 1962. It was razed in 1982 or 1983. Angelo's daughter, Nancy Knape, has her beauty shop on the land where the Rose Garden once stood.

FEC # 207 Photo of Rose Garden being demolished. Courtesy Angelo Tramuto.

FEC # 208 Photo of Rose Garden being demolished. Courtesy Angelo Tramuto.

ROSE GARDEN CLUB

DICKINSON, TEXAS

FEC # 209 Rose Garden menu. Courtesy Angelo Tramuto.

TAKE OUR DICE HOME WITH YOU

Ask For Them After A Hand Is Over

FEC # 210 Sign from the Rose Garden. Courtesy Angelo Tramuto.

FEC # 211 Nancy Knape's beauty shop and her commemorative "Rose Garden."

FEC # 212 OBV. & REV. Black.

FEC # 213 OBV. & REV. Pink.

FEC # 214 OBV. & REV. Red.

FEC # 215 OBV. & REV. Blue.

FEC # 216 OBV. & REV. White.

FEC # 217 OBV. & REV. Tan.

Roseland Supper Club

Reported to be 61st St. and Stewart Rd., Galveston, owner/operator, unknown.

Sea Club

Kemah, owner/operator, unknown. I got the chips from a man Dickinson, he said that the club was in Kemah.

FEC # 218 OBV. & REV. Rose.

FEC # 219 OBV. & REV. Green.

Seahorse Club

Seahorse Hotel, Galveston. Note the membership card is for the same Capt. A. W. Durrett as the Golden Greek.

MEMBERSHIP CARD B 360
SEAHORSE CLUB
SEAHORSE HOTEL
GALVESTON, TEXAS
is is to certify that
Capt. A. W. Durrett
is a member of The Seahorse Club and is entitled to the benefits and privileges of membership.
Mrs A. W. Durrett
Member's Signature

FEC # 220 Membership card.

FEC # 221 Plastic drink stir stick.

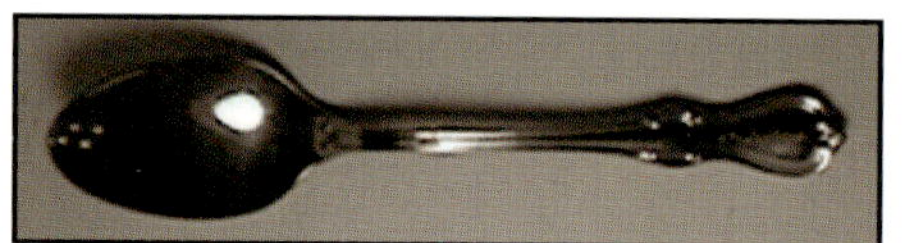

FEC # 222 Spoon from Seahorse.

Seaview Cafe

2502 Seawall Blvd., Galveston, owner/operator, Mack S. and James M. Cokins.

FEC # 223-A Matchbook, back.

FEC # 223-B Matchbook, front.

Seven Seas

2109½ Ave. C, Galveston, owner/operator, Ernest Hill.

FEC # 224 Ad April 4, 1947.
Galveston Week.

"7" SEAS

★

Watch for Opening
Of Gala Spring Show

★

CONTINUOUS MUSIC
AND DANCING

ERNEST HILL, Mgr.

2109½ Ave. C Ph. 2-7760

Seventy Five

Hwy. 3, Dickinson, owner/operator, George Harris.

FEC # 225 OBV. & REV. Yellow.

FEC # 226 OBV. & REV. Tan.

Shadowland Night Club

Blanco Rd., Galveston, owner/operator, Earl "Butter" Ramsey, 1920's. Earl also owned Southern Club.

Ship Ahoy Club

608½ 22nd St., Galveston, owner/operator, Thomas J. Golias.

FEC # 227 OBV. & REV. Tan.

Shipmate's Club

Galveston, owner/operator, Charles J. and Peggy Rowley. It was raided on 6/13/57.

Ship's Light Club

214 20th St., Galveston, owner/operator, Al and Marie A. Cherepica.

Shorthorn Club

213 22nd St., Galveston, owner/operator, E. Irene Kelly.

Siliva D

Kemah, owner/operator, unknown, Some old cronies in Dickinson told me about the club.

Silver Moon

Hwy. 3 and Deats Rd., Dickinson, owner/operator, Samuel T. Maceo, the Emmite brothers, the Salvato brothers, and Carlo Falco. The restaurant would seat about 50 people, they had two dice tables, a roulette wheel, and slot machines. There were small motel-type buildings along the side of the building, they called "tourist courts." Edna Sedgewick, Sam's wife, and Christie Mitchell got into a dance contest. All of the other contestants were Arthur Murray students, the judges were Arthur Murray instructors. Edna and Christie won the Rumba contest. The 1st prize was just what they really needed, a weekend in Galveston. Pinky Hull told me a story about him playing there one night during a hurricane.

FEC # 228 OBV. & REV. Tan.

FEC # 229 OBV. & REV. Orange.

FEC # 230 OBV. & REV. White.

FEC # 229 was a $5 chip with the five ground down and a one scratched in it place. It was also painted silver. The man I got it from said he had six or seven and they were all the same way.

FEC # 231 Ad from July 18, 1952.
Galveston Week.

FEC # 232 Photo of Silver Moon, up for sale. Courtesy Vern Blanck. Circa early 1990's.

FEC # 233 Photo of Silver Moon after fire and vandals, and just before being razed. There is now a convenience store on the lot. Circa 1996.

FEC # 234-A Matchbook, front.

FEC # 234-B Matchbook, back.

FEC # 234-C Matchbook, inside.

Southern Club

2728 61st St., Galveston, owner/operator, Earl "Butter" Ramsey, 1951 City Directory. Earl also owned the Shadowland Night Club. A March 3, 1948 Galveston Week shows Iris and Al as operators of club.

FEC # 235-A OBV. Yellow.

FEC # 235-B REV.

Sportsmans Club

Broadway and 68th St., Galveston, owner/operator, TAC, Harry Alexander, and Frank Pinto. Was one of the 47 night spots listed in the June 11, 1957 injunctions. Gambling and bingo.

FEC # 236 Glass reads Sportsmans Club Galveston, Texas. Covers the entire 68th block on Broadway.

Star Drug Store

510-512 23rd St., Galveston, owner/operator, William A. Hughes and George W. Clampitt. The Star took bets for Maceos.

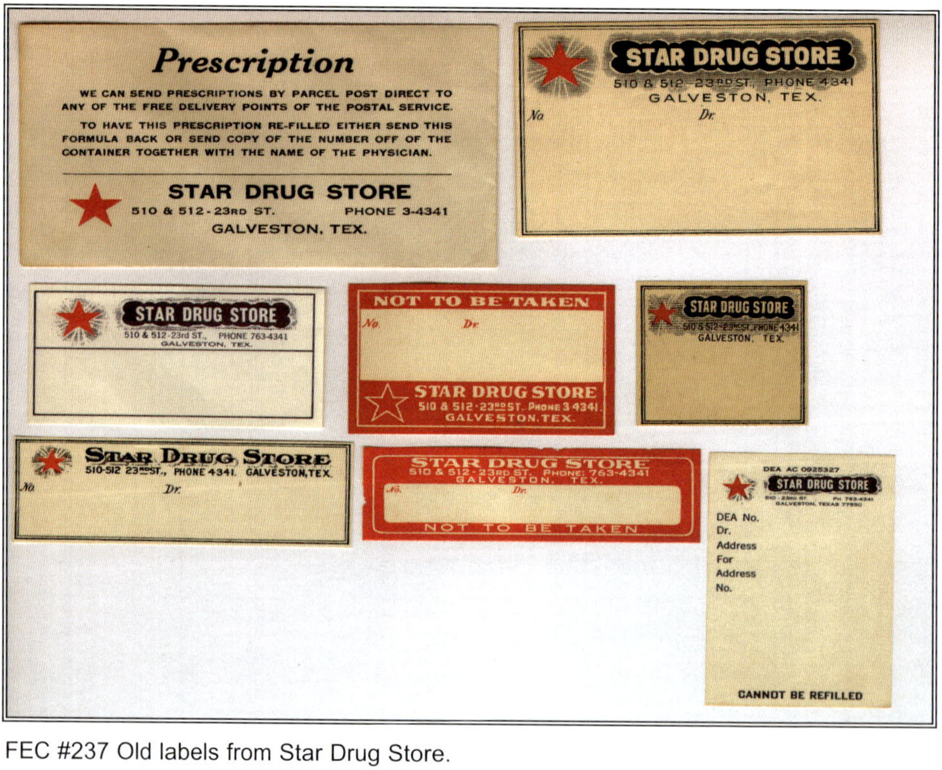

Prescription

WE CAN SEND PRESCRIPTIONS BY PARCEL POST DIRECT TO ANY OF THE FREE DELIVERY POINTS OF THE POSTAL SERVICE.

TO HAVE THIS PRESCRIPTION RE-FILLED EITHER SEND THIS FORMULA BACK OR SEND COPY OF THE NUMBER OFF OF THE CONTAINER TOGETHER WITH THE NAME OF THE PHYSICIAN.

STAR DRUG STORE
510 & 512 - 23RD ST. PHONE 3-4341
GALVESTON, TEX.

STAR DRUG STORE
510 & 512 23RD ST. PHONE 4341
GALVESTON, TEX.
No Dr.

STAR DRUG STORE
510 & 512-23rd ST., PHONE 763-4341
GALVESTON, TEX.

NOT TO BE TAKEN
No. Dr.
STAR DRUG STORE
510 & 512-23RD ST. PHONE 3 4341
GALVESTON, TEX.

STAR DRUG STORE
510 & 512-23RD ST. PHONE 4341
GALVESTON, TEX.

STAR DRUG STORE
510-512 23RD ST., PHONE 4341. GALVESTON, TEX.
No Dr.

STAR DRUG STORE
510 & 512-23RD ST. PHONE: 763-4341
GALVESTON, TEX.
No. Dr.
NOT TO BE TAKEN

DEA AC 0925327
STAR DRUG STORE
DEA No.
Dr.
Address
For
Address
No.
CANNOT BE REFILLED

FEC #237 Old labels from Star Drug Store.

STAR DRUG STORE

BREAKFAST

1 Egg with Choice of Ham or Bacon or Sausage	.40¢
2 Eggs with Choice of Ham or Bacon or Sausage	.50¢
All Cereals	.25¢
Half Order Toast, Butter, Jelly	.10¢
Full Order	.15¢
Raisin Toast	.15¢

JUICES

Large Orange Juice	30¢
Small Orange Juice	20¢
Large Grapefruit	30¢
Small Grapefruit Juice	20¢
Large GrapeJuice, Straight	30¢
Small Grape Juice, Straight	20¢
Large Tomato Juice	30¢
Small Tomato Juice	20¢
Large Pineapple Juice	30¢
Small Pineapple Juice	20¢

FEC # 238 Old menu, note prices.

SANDWICHES

Bar-B-Cue	35¢
Open Face Grilled Cheese	30¢
Ham	35¢
Roast Beef	35¢
Roast Pork	.35¢
Bacon	.35¢
Sausage	.30¢
Cheese	.30¢
Chicken Salad	.30¢
Ham Salad	.30¢
Egg Salad	.30¢
Pimento Cheese	.30¢
Tuna Fish	.35¢
Goose Liver	.30¢
Sliced Chicken	.50¢
Grilled Cheese	.30¢
Peanut Butter & Jelly	.30¢
Club	.75¢
All Combination Sandwiches	.50¢

MARGARINE SERVED HERE

Stewart Beach

Seawall Blvd. and 4th St., Galveston, owner/operator, Eddie Giusti. It had bingo and many forms of games of chance.

FEC # 239 Ad from November 3, 1950. Galveston Week.

Stork Club

2002 Ave. E, Galveston, owner/operator, Alf J. DelPapa. The 1955 City Directory listed Alf J. DelPapa and the Corral Club at this address. Was one of the 47 night spots listed in the June 11, 1957 injunctions. Gambling and liquor.

Streamline Dinner Club

Algoa on the Houston-Alvin Hwy., owner/operator, TAC, S. T. Maceo, Philip Barbaria of Dickinson, and Carlo Falco. They had three dice tables, one roulette wheel, horse bets, and slot machines. Was one of the 47 night spots listed in the June 11, 1957 injunctions. Gambling and liquor. They were also hit in the mop-up raids on 6/13/57. A friend of mine told me that she was at the Streamline Dinner Club one night when it was raided by the Rangers. She said it was a very quiet raid and that if you weren't paying attention, you wouldn't have known there was a raid taking place. She said that she didn't know the date, but she remembered that the club was open for quite awhile after the raid. From what I have been told the Streamline Dinner Club was one of the nicest clubs on the mainland. It had superb food and some of the best bands and entertainers in the business.

FEC # 240 OBV. & REV. Dark red with four yellow painted water marks on rim.

FEC # 241 OBV. & REV. No water marks.

FOR THE BEST STEAKS IN TEXAS
AND
FOR THE FINEST MUSIC

DINE AND DANCE AT THE

Matchless

STREAMLINE
DINNER CLUB

TO THE MUSIC OF

JOSÉ «MR. PIANO» ORTIZ
AND HIS ORCHESTRA

CLOSED ON MONDAYS

In Algoa on the
Houston-Alvin Highway

For Reservations
101J2 or 117

FEC # 242 Full page ad from November 3, 1950. Galveston Week.

Studio Lounge

2216 Market, P. O. Box 329, Galveston, owner/operator, TAC, various Maceos and Fertittas. Sheriff Paul Hopkins visited the Turf Grill on May 30, 1957 and told Vic Fertitta he wanted to go up to the Studio Lounge. They entered the very slow elevator and headed toward the second floor. The alarm work as it was supposed to, but two of the gamblers turned out to be lawmen and they stopped them from hiding the gambling equipment. The bartender and manager were charged with promoting gambling. It was damaged and temporarily closed by a fire in March 1948.

ANNOUNCEMENT

Studio Lounge, your downtown clubrooms, was damaged during a recent fire in the Turf Building. An extensive remodeling and redecorating program is now in progress. The reopening date will be announced in the verv near future.

•

STUDIO LOUNGE

In Downtown Galveston

2216 Market St.

FEC # 243 Ad from March 1948. Galveston Isle Magazine.

FEC # 244 Photo of Mary Hatcher at Studio Lounge, June 9, 1950. Galveston Isle Magazine.

FOR A PRIVATE PARTY

Invite Your Friends to The Beautiful Studio Lounge

★ ★ ★

Studio Lounge, whose T. A. C. clubrooms formally closed for the Winter season on September 1st, is now available for private parties and banquets. A competent staff will care for your every party need and handle all arrangements.

For estimates and information, call 2-9661 or write Catering Manager, P. O. Box 329, Galveston, Texas.

●

STUDIO LOUNGE
In Downtown Galveston
2216 Market Street

FEC # 245 Full page ad from November 1947. Galveston Isle Magazine.

FEC # 246 Photo of inside the Studio Lounge. Courtesy of Rosenberg Library, Galveston, Texas.

FEC # 247 Cover of menu from Studio Lounge. Courtesy of Rosenberg Library, Galveston, Texas.

I stopped by a store on Westheimer, to pick up a calendar from a local radio station that was having a promo there. While I was in the store, I met Paul Berlin, the renowned radio personality from KQUE 102.9 F M in Houston. We were talking while Paul was autographing a calendar for my wife and the subject of my book came up. With Paul being in the entertainment business, I began to pick his brain, something I usually do with anyone who might have a magnificent, untold story about Galveston.

Paul told me the following story. It happened in July or August of 1950, just before his twenty-first birthday in August. Please, don't get out your calculators. Paul was with a friend from Memphis. They were at the Studio Lounge in Galveston and began shooting craps. Paul admitted to me that he was not that knowledgeable about craps and wasn't sure just where to place the bets. His buddy would hold the chips and place the bets and it was Paul's job to shoot the dice. Seven-come-eleven, them dice got HOT! Paul said they were on a winning streak that wouldn't quit. When they cashed in their chips, Paul had won enough money, shy about $200, to pay cash for a brand new 1950 Ford convertible, which he purchased on his return to Houston.

Consistently seeking more information to be used in my book, I ask Paul a few more questions about the decor of the Turf Grill Building and the Studio Lounge. He said he didn't remember all that much about the place. But when I ask him what color his new car was, he answered me, in less than a heartbeat. "It was dark blue with red seat covers!"

FEC # 248 Napkin from Studio.

FEC # 249 Demitasse cup and saucer.

FEC # 250 The nine scenes on this page are from a Studio Lounge tablecloth.

FEC # 251 OBV. & REV. Purple.

FEC # 252 OBV. & REV. Black.
Courtesy Angelo Montalbano.

FEC # 253 OBV. & REV. Orange.

FEC # 254 OBV. & REV. Tan.

FEC # 255 OBV. & REV. Tan.

Also see the deck of cards under Balinese Room, FEC # 41 A, B, C, D, that have Studio Lounge on them. The Studio Lounge was the swank place to be seen. Many large social and business organizations had luncheons, meetings, and conventions there. Many of the entertainers that played the Balinese Room and the Marine Room also stared at the Studio Lounge. It was known for its originate zebra furniture. The E. S. Levey & Co. use to put on style shows at the Studio Lounge.

Sui Jen

2107 Seawall Blvd. at 21st St., Galveston, owner/operator, Sam and Rose Maceo. It was opened as the Chop Suey in 1923, then became Maceo's Grotto in 1926. Damaged by a hurricane in 1932, remodeled and reopened as the Sui Jen, (pronounced Swee Wren), in the same year, then became the Balinese Room in 1942.

FEC # 256 Chop sticks that read, Sui Jen Cafe, Galveston, Tex. They have a red ribbon and I was told that they were given away on the opening night of the Sui Jen.

FEC # 257 OBV. & REV. Red. This is the only design and dollar amount ever seen.

FEC # 258 Double sided placard. See Hollywood Dinner Club # 143 for other side.

Surf Social Club

628 Ave. K, Galveston, owner/operator, A. F. McBride. Houston Chronicle 3/2/41, "In Galveston on 3/1/41, A. F. McBride pleaded guilty of permitting gambling, fined $25 and court cost by Justice James A. Piperi. Charges filed by Texas Ranger J. A. Thompson.

T & C Club

Dickinson, owner/operator, unknown. Angelo Tramuto identified this chip for me. Angelo and Jim Simpson, both said it was short for the Town and Country Club.

FEC # 259 OBV. & REV. Yellow.

TAC

The Turf Athletic Club was a partnership formed on 8/6/32 between Sam and Rose Maceo, Dutch Voight, Frank and D. D. Alexander. It was the holding company for the Maceo organization. Many items were made for use in any of the TAC restaurants, clubs, or other establishments. There were many TAC chips made. Some had the club's initials BR or SL, or the name Balinese Room, Western Room, or Turf Club to name a few. Others had just TURF or TAC. These chip could be used in any of the Maceo clubs. I have been told by many that the TAC chip would be taken for cash at many stores, filling stations, eating establishments, and for private debts. Their chips were as good as gold.

FEC # 260 Small glass. No markings. There is a larger glass, where the ball has a light green tint. Courtesy Angelo Montalbano.

FEC # 261 10½" dinner plate with gold trim.

FEC # 262 7½" luncheon plate with gold trim.

FEC # 263 Cup. No initials.

FEC # 264 Saucer. No initials.

FEC # 265 TAC silverware. L to R
Gumbo spoom, TURF A.C. on REV.
Oyster fork, TAC on OBV.
Demitasse spoon TAC on OBV.

FEC # 266 Paper drink cup with 11 scenes.
Stewart Beach Park, Murdoch's Amusement,
Turf Tap Room, Beach Amusement,
Turf Grill Outside, Turf Grill Inside,
Studio Lounge, Balinese Room Outside,
The Corner, Balinese Room Inside,
The Fish House.

FEC # 267 No, it's not a silver happy face with glasses. It's a silver tray with a salt and pepper shaker holder. TURF A.C. on bottom.

FEC # 268 Silver shrimp cocktail server. TURF A.C. on top ring.

FEC # 269 OBV. & REV. Black.

FEC # 270 OBV. & REV. Orange.

FEC # 271 OBV. & REV. Tan.

Tennis Club

2706 Ave. Q, Galveston, owner/operator, Jesse Castilla.

FEC # 272 Ad from April 4, 1947. Galveston Week.

TENNIS CLUB
See You After the Game
2706 Avenue Q
PHONE 4844
Jesse Castilla, Mgr.

The Corner

21st St. and Ave. C, Galveston, owner/operator, TAC, Sam Maceo.

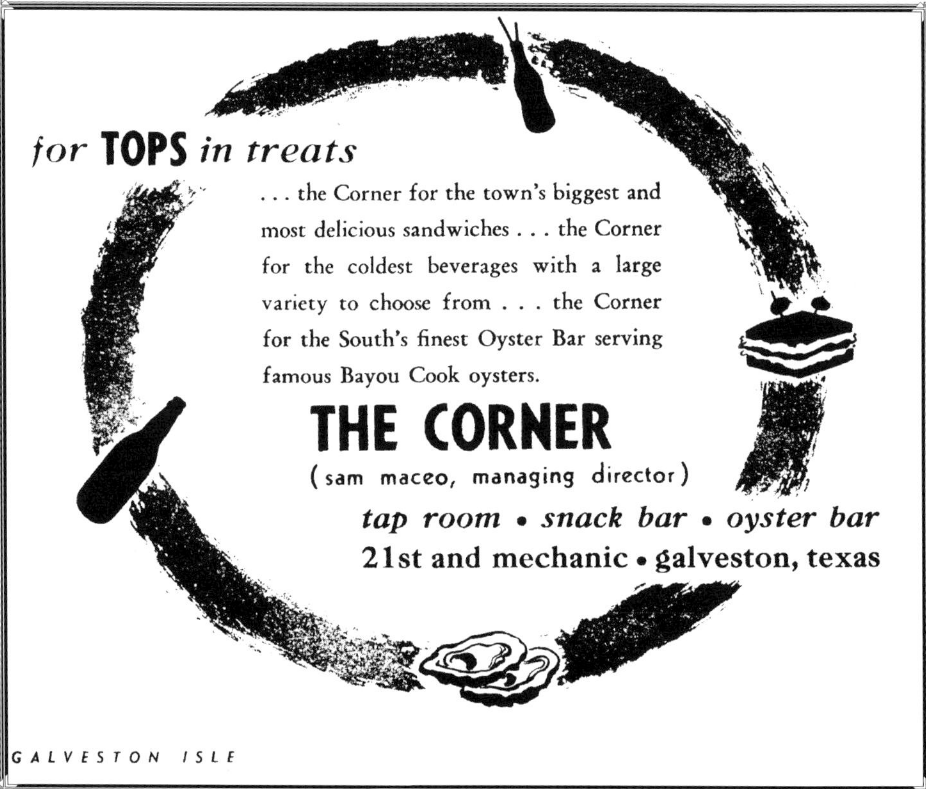

FEC # 273 Ad from June 1950. Galveston Isle Magazine.

Tipo Club

2604 Ave. D, Galveston, owner/operator, Charles T. Long. The 1955 City Directory listed Charles T. Long as the householder of Mother Harvey's, aka the Mollie Walters House, 2528 Postoffice Ave E.

Top Hat

Hwy. 6, Algoa, owner/operator, unknown. It was described as a very plush night club. The Top Hat was raided March 11, 1952, by the Texas Rangers, led by Eddie Oliver and Johnny Klevenhagen. They made twenty-one arrests and raked up about $5,000 for the gaming tables.

FEC # 274 OBV. & REV. Brown.

FEC # 275 OBV. & REV. Red.

FEC # 276 OBV. & REV. Rose pink.

Trade Winds Club

1913 22nd St., Galveston, owner/operator, Lee Woodson, William J. Hoover. Was one of the 47 night spots listed in the June 11, 1957 injunctions. Gambling and liquor.

Turf

These are four known turf chips used by the TAC.

FEC # 277 OBV. & REV. Black.

FEC # 278 OBV. & REV. Orange.

FEC # 279 OBV. & REV. Tan.

FEC # 280 OBV. & REV. Blue.

Turf Cigar Stand

210 Moody Ave., Galveston, owner/operator, TAC. During one of the raids, they found two hundred boxes of tip books.

Turf Club

2214 Ave. D, Galveston, owner/operator, TAC. The Turf Club was in their headquarters building downtown. It was on the second floor, with the Studio Lounge. It was opened in 1930, by Sam and Rose, and was still in open June 1957. The Turf was open 24 hours a day. You could bet on horse races and other sporting events. They had a professional billiards player on the staff, who took on all comers.

FEC # 281 OBV. & REV. Maroon.

Turf Grill

2216 Market, Ave D, Galveston, owner/operator, TAC, Tom (Tommie) A. Fertitta. The Turf Grill was the place to be when you were downtown. It was open 24 hours a day and had some of the best food in town. You could see any and everybody at the Grill, from a laborer to a judge, they all went there. There was an electric eye on the door for a while, but people would go in the wrong way and kept getting hit by the door. They removed it and replaced it with the first revolving door in Texas. There were poker games on the second floor, in the Turf Club, under the direction of Joe Megna. They sold tip books at the cigar stand. They also had tumbling, boxing, and other legitimate athletic activities on the third floor. The place was wrecked in 1935, by Texas Rangers, and had to be rebuilt. The building was razed in the 1970's and a bank now sets on the lot.

FEC # 282-A Old matches, front.

FEC # 282-B Old matches, back.

FEC # 283 Matchbook, front.
See Murdoch's # 182 for back.

FEC # 284 Menu from Turf Grill.

FEC # 285 Ad from September 1950. Galveston Isle Magazine.

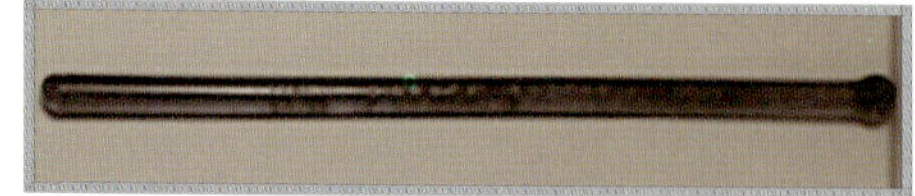
FEC # 286 Blue cobalt drink stir stick that reads.
TURF GRILL
2216 AVENUE D
GALVESTON, TEXAS

FEC # 287-A Matchbook, front.

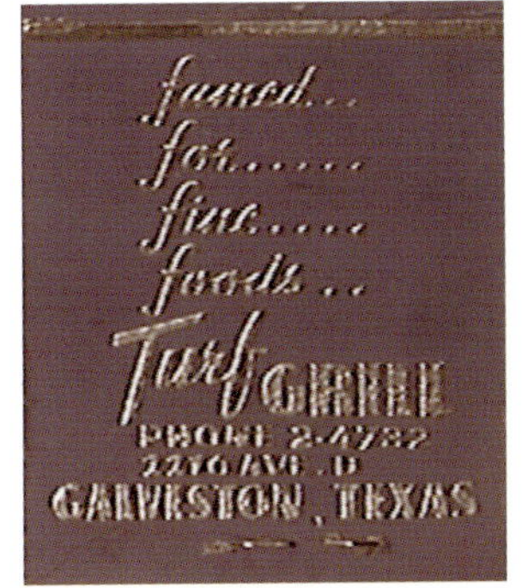

FEC # 287-B Matchbook, back.

FEC # 288 Gumbo bowl.

FEC # 289 Coffee cup.

FEC # 290 Demitasse cup.

FEC # 291 Demitasse saucer.

FEC # 292 Creamer.

FEC # 293 Mustard dish.

FEC # 294 Ceramic coffer cup.

FEC # 295 Copper soda holder.

FEC # 296 Gravy boat.

Turf Tap Room

2214 Market, Ave. D, Galveston, owner/operator, TAC. This was also located in the Turf Building.

FEC # 297 Matchbook, front.
See Murdoch's # 181 for back.

FEC # 298 Ad from September 1950. Galveston Isle Magazine.

2709½ Club

2709½ Market, Galveston, owner/operator, Jo Jo Hatch and Dottie Malone. Was one of the 47 night spots listed in the June 11, 1957 injunctions. Bawdy house and liquor violations.

U Club

2012 Ave. D, Galveston, owner/operator, Ross Christy and James A. Alexander, 1949 City Directory. The 1951 City Directory added Frank Grieves as owner/operator.

Uptown Club

2608½ Ave. D, Galveston, owner/operator, Betty Mitchell.

Villa Rose Dinner Club

Galveston, owner/operator, Dutch Voight. Early 1930's gambling spot.

Vincent C Bar

911 21st St., Galveston, owner/operator, William T. Evans.

FEC # 299 OBV. & REV. Dark red.

The Wagon Wheel

On 517, Dickinson, owner/operator, unknown. Had gambling.

Western Room

2216 Market, Ave. D, 3rd floor of the Turf Grill Building, owner/operator, TAC. It was opened 8/19/50 by Maceo and Co. Was one of the 47 night spots listed in the June 11, 1957 injunctions. Gambling (blackjack and dice) and liquor. It was also hit in the mop-up raids on 6/13/57. After Sam and Rose cashed in their chips and went to shoot craps in the clouds, Gulf Properties leased the Turf Grill, Western Room, and Balinese Room to cousins Anthony J. and Victor J. Ferittia, and Lorainsa Grillette.

FEC # 300 OBV. & REV. Tan with green water marks. This is the only known denomination in this chip design.

WESTERN
$25
ROOM

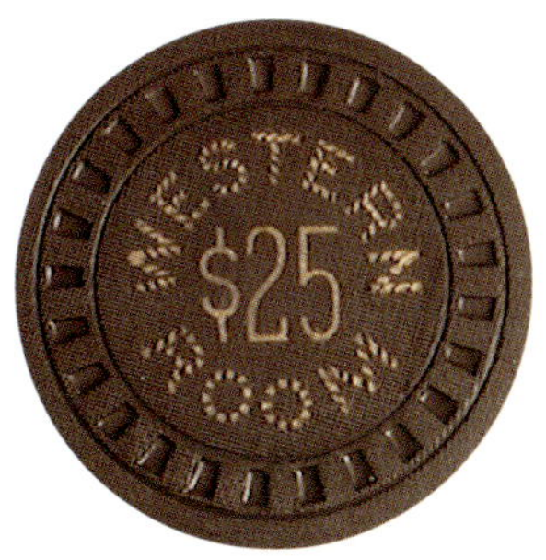

FEC # 301 OBV. & REV. Black.

$5

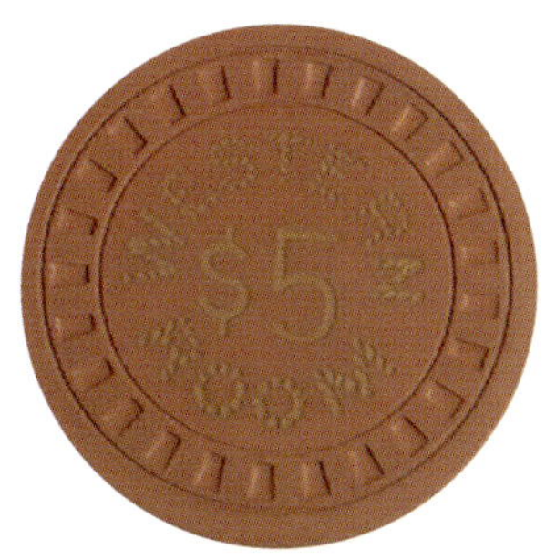

FEC # 302 OBV. & REV. Orange.

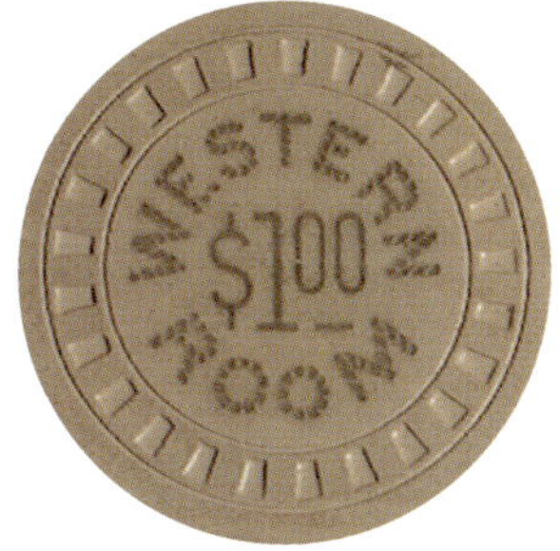

WESTERN
$1.00
ROOM

FEC # 303 OBV. & REV. Tan.

25¢

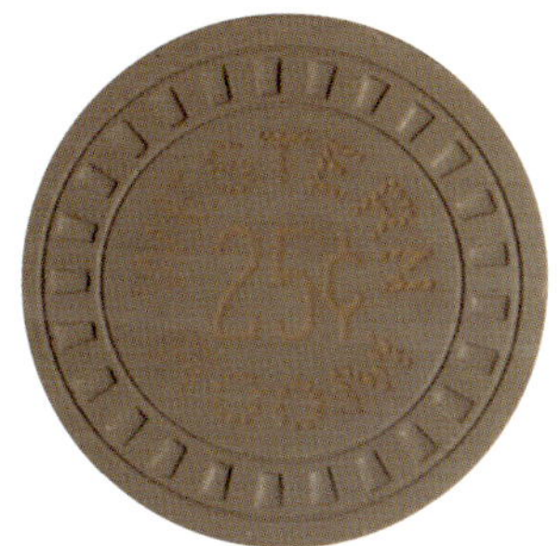

FEC # 304 OBV. & REV. Green.

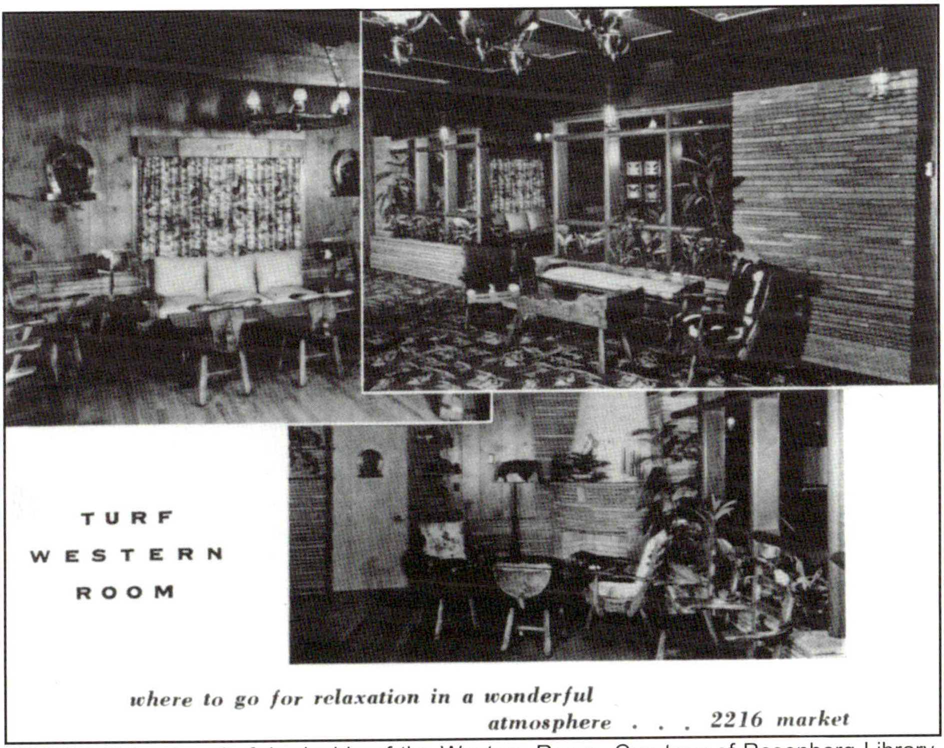
TURF
WESTERN
ROOM
where to go for relaxation in a wonderful
atmosphere . . . 2216 market

FEC # 305 Photo ad of the inside of the Western Room. Courtesy of Rosenberg Library, Galveston, Texas.

FEC # 306-A OBV. Blue.

FEC # 306-B REV.

FEC # 307-A OBV. Orange.

FEC # 307-B REV.

FEC # 308-A OBV. Tan.

FEC # 308-B REV.

FEC # 309-A OBV. Purple.

FEC # 309-B REV.

FEC # 310-A OBV. Blue.

FEC # 310-B REV.

FEC # 311-A OBV. Orange.

FEC # 311-B REV.

Wheel House

Kemah, owner/operator, unknown.

FEC # 312-A OBV. Green.

FEC # 312-B REV.

White House Club

2nd St., Kemah, owner/operator, unknown. It was a white house, that sat on stilts, on 2nd St., across the street from the Kemah Coffee Club.

FEC # 313 OBV. & REV. Blue.

FEC # 314 OBV. & REV. Yellow.

Yacht Balinese

This was Maceo's yacht. It was used for fishing and party trips for the family and VIP visitors to Galveston. I have heard from two different people, five years apart, of a chip that had Yacht Balinese on it, but I have never seen one. It may have had gambling, but I think it was on a private bases. This may have been the boat used in the business, Miss Hollywood Inc.

FEC # 315 L to R. Joe Maceo, Vincent Maceo, A. J. Adams, Robert Lee Fabj, crew member, and R. S. Maceo. November 1947. Galveston Isle Magazine.

FEC # 316 Ruth Barnhart and Julian Pace, from Waco, compare catches aboard the Yacht Balinese, March 6. March 1950. Galveston Isle Magazine.

ESTABLISHMENTS AROUND HOUSTON AND THE STATE

Castle Farm

San Antonio, owner/operator, unknown.

FEC # 317 OBV. & REV. Brown.

Castle Hills

San Antonio, owner/operator, Slim Lambert and Tom Moore.

FEC # 318 OBV. & REV. Rose. Black water marks.

FEC # 319 OBV. & REV. Blue.

Cork Club

Houston, in the Shamrock Hotel, owner/operator, Glenn McCarthy. It was opened March 17, 1949. Some of the stars that performed there were Dinah Shore, Frank Sinatra, Dean Martin, Rosemary Clooney, and Debbie Reynolds.

Anthony Fertitta went to Las Vegas for a short time, moved back to Houston and worked at Glenn McCarthy's Cork Club. He ended up in his hometown of Leesville, Louisiana, where, with his brother Sam, they entered into the home construction business and he was later elected mayor.

Domain Privee

Houston, South Main St., owner/operator, Jakie Freedman. Jakie was an investor in the Hollywood Dinner Club but sold his interest to the original partners in 1927. After selling out, Freedman moved to Houston, where he opened the elegant, colonial mansion, Domain Privee. When the gambling laws started being enforced in the early 1950's, he closed the Domain Privee and moved the Las Vegas where gambling was legal and ran the world famous Sands. Pinky Hull played there in Summer of 1946. See Domain Privee FEC # 3.

Dugout

Houston, South Main St., owner/operator, unknown. The Dugout was on the south side on Main St., beyond the Domain Privee and before the Green Light. When you went into the place you would go straight down a staircase into the basement. The building was just a facade. There was nothing upstairs.

Green Light

Stafford, just southwest of Houston, on South Main St., owner/operator, Gene Allison.

FEC # 320-A OBV. Green.

FEC # 320-B REV.

FEC # 321-A OBV. Red.

FEC # 321-B REV.

H O B

San Antonio, owner/operator, H. O. "Red" Berry. Berry was one of the big time operators, who later became a politician and served as a legislature from Sam Antonio.

FEC # 322 OBV. & REV. Brown.

FEC # 323 OBV. & REV. Dark red.

FEC # 324 OBV. & REV. Black.

FEC # 325 OBV. & REV. Yellow.

Houston Casino

Houston, 3333 Sage, owner/operator, unknown. The place had mock gambling. It is now closed.

FEC # 326 OBV. & REV.
Aluminum, pink.

FEC # 327 OBV. & REV.
Aluminum, blue.

FEC # 328 OBV. & REV.
Aluminum, clear.

FEC # 329 OBV. & REV.
Aluminum, purple.

FEC # 330 OBV. & REV. Light blue.

FEC # 331 OBV. & REV. Blue.

FEC # 332 OBV. & REV. Yellow.

FEC # 333 OBV. & REV. Pink.

FEC # 334 OBV. & REV. Black.

Manhattan Cafe

Victoria, owner/operator, unknown.

FEC # 335-A Matchbook, front.

FEC # 335-B Matchbook, back.

Otters Club

Houston, 718 McKinney, owner/operator, Mr. Sullivan. A 1930's gambling casino, it is now the Tenneco Building.

Southern Dinner Club

Houston, 807 Gray, owner/operator, unknown.

FEC # 336-A Matchbook, front.

FEC # 336-B Matchbook, inside.

FEC # 336-C Matchbook, back.

Sylvan Club

Rosenberg, owner/operator, unknown.

FEC # 337-A Matchbook, front.

FEC # 337-B Matchbook, inside.

FEC # 337-C Matchbook, back.

Vernon Country Club

Vernon, northwest of Dallas, owner/operator, unknown.

FEC # 338-A OBV. Yellow. Gray water marks.

FEC # 338-B REV.

FEC # 339-A OBV. Orange. Black water marks.

FEC # 339-B REV.

I have only named a few of the casinos from around the state. There were many other club in the Houston, San Antonio, and Dallas that had gambling. Texas was one of the hot beds in the nation for gambling.

NEAT GALVESTON STUFF

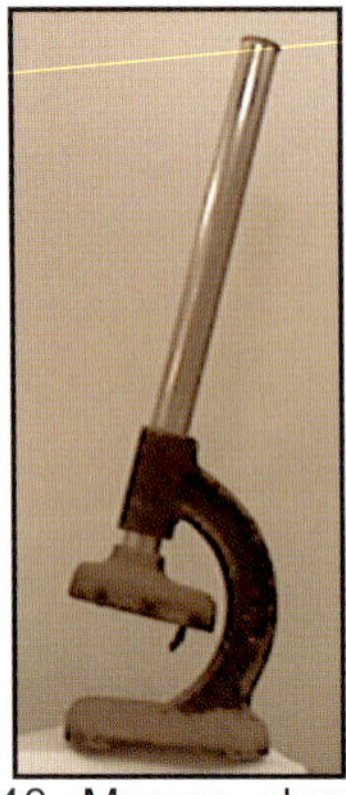

FEC # 340 Money changer, 18" high. You get five nickels a pull. This was used in three different Galveston clubs, but I lost the note as to which clubs they were.

FEC # 341 Souvenir of Galveston. Potmetal glass holder with five scenes of Galveston.

FEC # 342 Souvenir cup and saucer with beach front scene.

FEC # 343 Wallet that has R. S. MACEO SEAFOODS, INC. GALVESTON, TEXAS on it.

FEC # 344 Glass domed paper weight with beach front scenes showing Crystal Palace. I got it at an antique show in Houston, from a dealer from the Midwest. What goes around comes around.

UNIDENTIFIED CHIPS

If the chip has a dollar amount on reverse, I have indicated as much. If I have it in a different color, that color is also listed.

FEC # 345 Maroon. Unknown.
GREEN TAVERN

FEC # 346 Deep red. Unknown.
MANOR

FEC # 347 Dark red. Unknown.
DELTA CLUB

FEC # 348 Lavender. Unknown.
BROOK CLUB

FEC # 349 Yellow-$1. Unknown.
OIL PATCH

FEC # 350 Yellow & Brown. Unknown.
THUNDERBIRD

FEC # 351 Red. Unknown.
DUCK

FEC # 352 Brown & Green. Unknown.
SWED

FEC # 353 Yellow. Unknown.
WEN

FEC # 354 Yellow. Unknown.
JHP

FEC # 355 Brown. Unknown.
EB

FEC # 356 Blue. Unknown.
FB

FEC # 357 Black. Unknown.
JMT

FEC # 358 Blue & Green. Unknown.
CB

FEC # 359 Light orange. Unknown.
CB

FEC # 360 Red & Tan. Unknown.
MNJ

FEC # 361 Lavender. Unknown.
A

FEC # 362 Orange & Green. Unknown.
ABK

FEC # 363 Red & Blue. Unknown.
DTL

FEC # 364 Brown. Unknown.
JHC

FEC # 365 Yellow. Unknown.
MT

FEC # 366 Rose & Brown. Unknown.
AC

FEC # 367 Brown. Unknown.
XX IN A HORSESHOE

FEC # 368 Flesh. Unknown.
FM

FEC # 369 Tan. Unknown.
CDF

FEC # 370 Green. Unknown.
HYC

FEC # 371 Yellow & Blue. Unknown.
TSW

FEC # 372 Blue, 4 designs. Unknown.
JBJ

FEC # 373 Purple. Unknown.
HM

FEC # 374 Burgundy. Unknown.
TIM

FEC # 375 Yellow. Unknown.
BMC

FEC # 376 Green. Galveston.
MD

FEC # 377 Black-$100. Kemah.
SHRIMP BOAT

FEC # 378 Red. Kemah.
STAR

FEC # 379 Tan. Galveston.
MOW

FEC # 380 Tan. Galveston.
RL

FEC # 381 Tan. Galveston.
W and B

FEC # 382 Blue & Red. Galveston. These chips came out of a Maceo warehouse.
ECM

FEC # 383 Tan. Galveston.
HNS

FEC # 384 Orange & Black. Galveston.
WD

FEC # 385 Pink-$1 & Yellow-$5. Unknown.
JSR

FEC # 386 Yellow. Unknown.
HORSE IN HORSESHOE

FEC # 387 Hot pink. Galveston.
GBC

FEC # 388 Red plastic. Unknown.
K

FEC # 389 Green. Galveston.
EAGLE

FEC # 390 Blue. Galveston.
$100

FEC # 391 Maroon. Unknown.
3 IN DIAMOND

FEC # 392 Maroon. Unknown.
8 IN CIRCLE